*Savoring the Peace of Jesus
in a Chaotic World*

THE GOSPEL OF John

FOR TEEN GIRLS

Melissa Spoelstra

Lifeway Press®
Brentwood, Tennessee

Published by Lifeway Press® • © 2024 Melissa Spoelstra

ISBN: 978-1-4300-9546-0 • Item: 005847612
Dewey decimal classification: 248.83
Subject headings: YOUNG ADULT NONFICTION / Religion / Biblical Stories & Studies

To order additional copies of this resource, write to Lifeway Resources Customer Service; 200 Powell Place, Suite 100; Brentwood, TN 37027-7707; order online at www.lifeway.com; fax 615.251.5933; phone toll free 800.458.2772; or email orderentry@lifeway.com.

Printed in the United States of America

Lifeway Students Bible Studies • Lifeway Resources
200 Powell Place, Suite 100 • Brentwood, TN 37027-7707

EDITORIAL TEAM, LIFEWAY WOMEN BIBLE STUDIES

Becky Loyd
Director, Lifeway Women

Tina Boesch
Manager

Chelsea Waack
Production Leader

Mike Wakefield
Content Editor

Lindsey Bush
Production Editor

Lauren Ervin
Art Director

Sarah Hobbs
Graphic Designer

EDITORIAL TEAM, LIFEWAY STUDENTS BIBLE STUDIES

Chuck Peters
Director, Lifeway NextGen

Karen Daniel
Manager, Small Group Resources

Amanda Mejias
Content Editor

Morgan Hawk
Production Editor

Shiloh Stufflebeam
Graphic Designer

Contents

About the Author   4

How To Use   6

SESSION ONE
INTRODUCTION TO THIS STUDY   8

SESSION TWO
PEACE IN THE PLAN OF JESUS   12

SESSION THREE
PEACE IN THE POWER OF JESUS   40

SESSION FOUR
PEACE IN THE PATIENCE OF JESUS   68

SESSION FIVE
PEACE IN THE PURPOSES OF JESUS   94

SESSION SIX
PEACE IN THE PROMISES OF JESUS   122

SESSION SEVEN
PEACE IN THE PASSION OF JESUS   148

Leader Guide   174

Extra Resources   178

Endnotes   188

Video Redemption Information   192

About the Author

Melissa Spoelstra is a women's conference speaker, Bible teacher, and author who is madly in love with Jesus and passionate about studying God's Word and helping women of all ages to seek Christ and know Him more intimately through serious Bible study. Melissa has a degree in Bible theology and is the author of the Bible studies *Isaiah: Striving Less and Trusting God More*; *Acts: Awakening to God in Everyday Life*; *The Names of God: His Character Revealed*; *Romans: Good News that Changes Everything*; *Elijah: Spiritual Stamina in Every Season*; *Numbers: Learning Contentment in a Culture of More*; *First Corinthians: Living Love When We Disagree*; *Joseph: The Journey to Forgiveness*; and *Jeremiah: Daring to Hope in an Unstable World*. She has also authored several books, including *Dare to Hope*; *Total Family Makeover: 8 Practical Steps to Making Disciples at Home*; and *Total Christmas Makeover: 31 Devotions to Celebrate with Purpose*. She is a regular contributor to the Proverbs 31 First Five App and the Girlfriends in God online daily devotional. Melissa lives in Waxahachie, Texas, with her pastor husband, Sean, and has four grown children: Zach, Abby, Sara, and Rachel.

FOLLOW MELISSA

Twitter	@MelSpoelstra
Instagram	@Melissa.Spoelstra
Facebook	/AuthorMelissaSpoelstra
Website	MelissaSpoelstra.com

A Letter
FROM MELISSA

Four of my immediate five family members are more than six feet tall. When our family is walking together, I often have to request them to slow down because I can't keep up with my tall tribe. I want to enjoy being with them, but if they don't slow down, I'll miss out on the conversation and their presence.

While I desire that slower pace with my family, I am often the one running ahead in my relationship with God. I can get moving pretty fast answering texts, going place to place, and checking off my to-do list. What about you? Is something preventing you from slowing down with Jesus lately?

Through the pages of the Gospel of John, my invitation for you is to slow your pace in order to experience the peace of Jesus in a chaotic world. In our culture filled with noise, screens, and busy schedules, we can fail to embrace the gift of peace Jesus promised. I often find myself worried about yesterday's problems and fearful of future ones. I don't want to give chaos authority in my life when Jesus offers me peace, but I wonder what it looks like to embrace His gift in the midst of a hectic life.

Jesus warned us that the world cannot give the kind of peace of heart and mind He spoke about (John 14:27). This peace involves stillness of soul rather than circumstantial ease. But how do we receive this gift of peace? No summer vacation, day at the spa, or Uber Eats® delivery can supply it.

Sometimes I think peace will appear when troubles disappear—when your room is clean, the friendship is mended, the final is over, and so forth. Yet, Jesus doesn't define *peace* this way. He says we can have peace—assurance of our salvation through Christ—in the midst of the trials and difficulties we have in this world.

Does that sound good to anyone else? Then I hope you'll meet me in the pages of John!

How to Use

Consider the following options and prayerfully decide what will
be the right fit for your current season and situation.

BASIC STUDY.

You can do this on your own or with a group.
The basic study includes five days of content
that combine study of Scripture with personal
reflection and application. This includes
looking up Scripture, reflecting, engaging in
interactive activities, and answering questions.

At the end of each day, you'll find a Stop and
Savor portion featuring reflection questions and
a prayer.

If you're a leader, I'm so
glad you're here! We have
a guide in the back of this
book on page 174 to help give
you some guidance as you
lead your group of girls.

If you feel up to more study, here are a few ideas
I recommend to add to your time in this study. You can pick
one or more:

WATCH the intro videos that accompany each session.
You have access to video teachings that provide additional
content to help you better understand and apply what you
just studied in the previous session. Information on how
to stream your videos can be found on page 192.

DISCUSS your study with a group of friends. You can
use the questions and prompts provided on the Group
Session pages to help you review the previous five days of
study and discuss the intro teaching together.

MEMORIZE the weekly Bible verses. It is helpful to recite
these verses with a partner, so pick one friend in your group
to get started.

KEEP IT SIMPLE.

Depending on your circumstances, you may
want to modify your goals. Perhaps it will be
a win if you attend group meetings, complete
three out of five days of study, or make some
other modification to your plan. Our desire
is not to check boxes but to savor the peace of
Jesus in our own lives. Pray for guidance and set
your goal accordingly.

1

Introduction

BEGIN

If you could only eat one flavor of ice cream for the rest of your life, what would it be?

Using the scale below, mark how familiar you are with the Gospels (Matthew, Mark, Luke, and John). Feel free to share your answer with the group.

Never Heard of Them   Kind of Familiar   Read All of Them!

On an ideal day, what does time alone with Jesus look like for you?

Circle the emotion that best describes how you feel about your time with God in recent weeks. Share your answer with the group.

Happy   Content   Anxious   Sad   Angry

If you could use any color to describe how you feel about life in general right now, what would it be? Why?

Choose one person to pray over the group and for your discussion time, that it would be beneficial for everyone and honoring to God.

REVIEW & DISCUSS

If you haven't yet, take time to watch the Session One video. (Instructions are in the back of your book.)

Look at the following three descriptions of the Gospel of John. Circle the numbers you already know, then underline which of these contains new information for you.

A. John is the brother of James.

B. The Gospel of John contains more than ninety percent unique content not found in the other Gospels (Matthew, Mark, and Luke).1

C. The Gospel of John was originally written to a Jewish audience.

Read John 20:30-31. Why did John say he wrote this Gospel?

Something you'll never see about Jesus in John (or in any of the Gospels) is that He was in a hurry or rushing from one thing to the next. Why do you think that is?

The Greek word for peace is *eirene* and has been defined as "the tranquil state of a soul assured of its salvation through Christ, and so fearing nothing from God and content with its earthly lot, of whatsoever sort that is."² Using that definition, how would you explain peace to a friend?

REFLECT & APPLY

What are the things that have stolen your peace recently?

In what area of your life do you wish you had more of God's peace?

Share a time when you have experienced God's peace.

What's one way you need to slow down this week in order to experience God's presence and peace?

Grab a note card, then write down this session's memory verse: John 1:12. Discuss one or two ways that will help you memorize this verse before the next group time.

 CLOSE

Read Philippians 4:6, then close using the following steps to lead you in prayer.

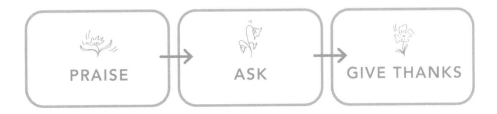

PRAISE → ASK → GIVE THANKS

Before Next Time }

HERE'S WHAT YOU'LL BE WORKING ON:
- Watch Session 2 Video
- Complete Session 2 Personal Study Days (as best you can!)
- Memorize John 1:12
- Stop and Savor

2

Peace in the Plan of Jesus

But to all who believed him and accepted him, he gave the right to become children of God.

John 1:12

Day One
A PRE-EXISTING PLAN

SCRIPTURE
FOCUS

John 1:1–34

BIG IDEA

Circumstances can feel confusing, but we can savor peace knowing that God established a plan before the beginning of time.

Life is a key theme in John's Gospel. He uses the Greek word for "life," zoe, thirty-six times!

I searched everywhere, but I could not find my car key. I mentally retraced my steps and deduced that I must have locked it in the car. My husband attempted to get into the vehicle by using a wire coat hanger with no success except to leave some permanent scratches. I then called a locksmith to open the car door, but once inside, we discovered the key was nowhere to be found. Eventually, we found it on the bathroom floor. I'd like to tell you this all happened calmly with no worry, hurry, or frustration. But that's not how it went down. At the end of the incident, I reflected on how pointless the whole situation seemed—damage done, money spent, and nothing to show for it.

Have you encountered a similar "seemingly pointless" situation? If so, jot a few sentences about your experience.

Trying to make sense of small frustrations like lost keys or more significant issues like physical pain, loss, or relational strain can rob us of peace. As we open the pages of the Gospel of John, we remember life is not random. Despite confusing circumstances, we can savor peace, knowing that God established a plan before the beginning of time. He is "always working" (John 5:17). Even when we don't feel it or see it, we can believe it.

THE WORD

Matthew began his Gospel with a genealogy connecting Joseph to Abraham, and Luke recorded the lineage of Jesus, tracing Mary's family tree to Adam. John reached back even further to Jesus's role in creation.

READ JOHN 1:1-5 and answer the following questions:

Who is "the Word" John referred to, and what do we find out about Him in these verses?

In your own words, summarize what is stated or implied about the Word's relationship to God, His existence, and His work.

The Greek word *Logos* labeling Jesus as the Word was used exclusively by John. His opening words are reminiscent of the book of Genesis and reveal the Son of God's role in creation. The Father accomplished His creative work through the Son (Col. 1:16; Heb. 1:2). John's wording also makes a statement about Jesus's eternal existence. He was not created, nor born. There has never been a time when He did not exist in community with the Father and the Holy Spirit.

John wrote in Revelation that Jesus is "Alpha" and "Omega"—the first and last letters of the Greek alphabet. (Rev. 1:8; 22:13). This was a definitive statement about Christ's eternality. He sees and knows the beginning and the end.

DWELT AMONG US

The deeper we know Jesus, the more we experience peace in His plan. READ JOHN 1:6-18 and record what Jesus did according to verse 14.

The Word "became human and made his home among us" (v. 14). Theologians refer to this action as the Incarnation. The verb used for "made his home" means "to pitch a tent, to dwell temporarily."[2] Jesus existed before creation but stepped into time and became one of us. He temporarily tabernacled among us on earth to live the perfect life we couldn't live and ultimately die on our behalf as the atoning sacrifice.

God put on flesh and came to earth to restore our broken relationship with Him. He came near.

Take a moment to savor His nearness. Fill in the blanks:

Jesus came to earth for _____ (my name) and is near in the midst of _____ (a challenging circumstance) in my life.

THE LAMB OF GOD

Jesus is the Word, the Life, the Light, and filled with grace and truth. His plan to redeem us meant He would lay down His life in exchange for ours.

READ JOHN 1:19-34 and summarize how John the Baptist described Jesus in the verses below:

Verse 29

Verse 30

Verse 34

From the beginning of Jesus's ministry, John the Baptist called Him the Lamb of God. The first readers of John's Gospel would have been familiar with the use of lambs for Jewish sacrifices, as commanded in the Old Testament. Each family had to have one for Passover (Ex. 12:1-10). When John the Baptist spoke this title over Jesus, he was foreshadowing Christ's sacrificial death to pay the penalty for my sin and yours.

Take a moment to reflect on the price Jesus paid on your behalf and thank Him for the right He has given you to become a child of God by believing in His name (John 1:12). Remember, no one is physically born a child of God. It happens by grace through faith (Eph. 2:1-10).

If you've placed your faith in Christ, share a brief paragraph about your experience. If you're not yet a follower of Christ, take some time to talk with your parents or a trusted adult from church about what that might look like. (I've also given you some information on page 179 that might help give you more understanding of what this means.)

John the Baptist and John, the author of this Gospel, are different individuals. John the Baptist was Jesus's cousin whose ministry preceded and prepared the way according to God's plan. John the author was the son of Zebedee and brother of James.

Whether your commitment to Christ began last week or years ago, our lives will hold pointless moments, complicated situations, and frustrating circumstances. Regardless, we can hold onto God's peace because He isn't stumbling through His calendar. His plan was conceived before time began—and that plan includes intimacy with Him!

As we walk through this study, we want to grow in experiencing God's peace. To help us do that, we'll wrap up each day by savoring what God revealed through John's Gospel about Jesus.

STOP AND SAVOR

Today we focused on this truth: *Circumstances can feel confusing, but we can savor peace knowing that God established a plan before the beginning of time.*

What's one thing you hope to remember about what you studied today?

As you reflect on today's passage, write down any words that stood out to you about who Jesus is.

Consider your life circumstances and complete the following sentence:

Because Jesus is Creator, the Word, Life, Light, full of grace and truth, and the Lamb of God who takes away my sin, I can experience peace in _____ _____.

Day Two
COME AND SEE

At restaurants I am often the first person at the table to decide what I want. As soon as I identify something that sounds good, I stop looking at the other choices. While this saves me from analysis paralysis, it also means I sometimes make hasty decisions.

Following Jesus means slowing down and considering our actions and decisions in light of His plan. We can't afford to choose our morality or devotion from the world's menu. Instead, we need to accept Jesus's invitation for us to come and see His plan for living.

WHAT DO YOU WANT?

The first followers of Jesus came to Him through the ministry of His cousin, John the Baptist.

READ JOHN 1:35-39 and draw a line to the person who said each statement:

"Look! There is the Lamb of God!" (v. 36).	*Jesus*
"What do you want?" (v. 38).	
"Rabbi, . . . where are you staying?" (v. 38).	*John's two disciples*
"Come and see" (v. 39).	*John the Baptist*

What stands out to you from this dialogue?

It's interesting that Jesus started the conversation by asking the two men following Him what they wanted. I mean, He's God—He knows everything. But His question helped them clarify their desires. They weren't looking for an address when they responded by asking where Jesus was staying. They called Him "Rabbi," which was a term of respect given to Jewish teachers that literally means, "Master."[3] Embedded in their question was a desire to be with Jesus and listen to His message.

Jesus didn't give them a detailed sermon about His incarnation (Him being both God and human). Instead, He invited them to "come and see"—not just so they could check out His lodging but to spend time with Him. He extends the same invitation to us, to be in a relationship with Him. We do that through the power of His Spirit, by obeying His Word, and in community with His people. He leads us as we make a myriad of decisions about our thoughts, attitudes, words, and actions. Understanding His purpose, instead of just leaning on our own understanding, helps us make sense of our circumstances.

> **Take a moment to respond to the words of Jesus from this passage. How do they resonate in your life?**
>
> *What do you want?*
>
> *Come and see.*

RESPONDING TO JESUS

READ JOHN 1:40-51 and record information given about the following people:

Andrew (vv. 40-42,44)

Peter (vv. 40-42,44)

Like Andrew and Peter, Philip was from Galilee and likely a fisherman. His hometown of Bethsaida literally means "house of fishing."[4]

Philip (vv. 43-45)

Nathanael (vv. 45-49)

What are some patterns or repeated phrases in the text?

Once people discovered Jesus, they wanted to bring their friends and relatives to Him. Philip even used Jesus's words in answering Nathanael's objections: "come and see."

Jesus didn't start His ministry with a big tent revival. He called individuals who then told others, who in turn told more people. Scholars surmise Nathanael was a student of Jewish law since Philip appealed to him by referencing Moses and the prophets. Jesus seemed to confirm that by stating He saw Nathanael under the fig tree. The fig tree phrase was used in rabbinic literature to describe meditation on the law.[5] In verse 51, Jesus referred to Jacob's vision of seeing a ladder (Gen. 28:10-17). He knew Nathanael, as a student of the Scriptures, was familiar with the story. Jesus was pointing to Himself as that stairway—the mediator between God and man.

Jesus didn't rush to accomplish His plan, revealing a portion at a time. He responded to seekers and sought out others, inviting them to come and see.

COME AND SEE

When it comes to following Jesus, we often want the whole plan laid out. Yet Jesus just says, "Come and see." He invites us into a deeper relationship—to know Him and learn from Him. Often, His words prompt me to respond similarly to King David's words in Psalm 27:8: "My heart has heard you say, 'Come and talk with me.' And my heart responds, 'Lᴏʀᴅ, I am coming.'" Other times my heart responds, but not with an eagerness to join Him. I'm busy, distracted, or overwhelmed.

What are some ways you might fill in this blank:

My heart responds, Lord, I am _____ .

Today, I've intentionally left some extra time to respond like King David. Use the next few minutes to think about Jesus's invitation to follow Him. Consider the following questions. Feel free to write responses or just think through them silently:

What helps you follow Jesus more closely?

What hinders you from following Him?

Is there anyone the Lord is prompting you to invite to "come and see"?

Now take some time to envision Jesus as the stairway between you and God. Write a prayer below, thanking Christ for being your mediator and asking Him to help you connect with Him more intimately through our study of the Gospel of John.

Jesus, you are the stairway to heaven. Thank you for inviting me to come and see. Thank you for the Gospel of John that allows me to know you more deeply. Help me to follow you more closely so I might walk according to your plans instead of mine. In Jesus's name, Amen.

STOP AND SAVOR

Today we focused on this truth: *We can savor peace when we respond to Jesus's invitation to come and see.*

What's one thing you hope to remember about what you studied today?

What did you notice about the plan and pace of Jesus in this passage?

How are you responding to Jesus's invitation to come and see?

Day Three

DO WHAT HE SAYS

As a pastor, my husband has officiated many weddings where things went wrong. Once he forgot to have the audience sit down, and they stood for the entire ceremony. Another time, a truck ran over the water main at the reception hall, leaving them with no water at the reception. These examples reveal that no matter how much you plan, unexpected things can and will happen!

> **I wonder if you have attended a wedding or special event where something went wrong. If something comes to mind, jot it below.**

THE PROBLEM

> **READ JOHN 2:1-3 and describe the problem that surfaced at the wedding in Cana.**

Running out of food or beverages at a wedding today would be embarrassing for the hosts. In biblical times, it was catastrophic. A groom could face a lawsuit over this lapse in hospitality.[6] And this kind of social embarrassment could have been joked about by people in their community for years.[7] I love how Mary chose to get involved, bringing the situation to Jesus.

I usually seek logical solutions in difficult situations. Often, I'll call a friend or mentor for advice. Other times I look to Google® or YouTube® for answers.

> **What are some ways you typically approach problems?**

BIG IDEA

If we desire the peace of Jesus, then we must do what He says.

Cana was about nine miles north of Nazareth where Jesus grew up, so it's possible His mother was a friend of the wedding family. Since there is no mention of Joseph, many scholars believe he had already died.[8]

For additional insights into Jewish weddings and funerals during the time of Jesus, check out the Digging Deeper article "Weddings and Funerals" found online at lifeway.com/gospelofjohn.

Like Mary, we need to bring the sticky situations we encounter directly to Jesus.

THE PLAN

READ JOHN 2:4-12 and answer the following questions:

What was Jesus's initial response to His mother's plea?

How did Mary instruct the servants?

What did Jesus reveal for the first time at this event (v. 11)?

While the other Gospel writers recorded more than forty miracles, John chose only seven to highlight. He referred to them as signs because they pointed to something significant.

Jesus referring to His mom as "woman" (v. 4) sounds almost rude through our cultural filters. But in His day this was a title of respect— like saying ma'am or madam.[9] Mary was His earthly mother, but He was shifting into public ministry and to His heavenly Father's business.

Jesus's response to Mary that His hour had not yet come is interesting. In ancient sources, one's hour or time referred to one's death. Scholar Craig Keener wrote, "Jesus may be saying, 'Once I begin performing signs, I start toward the cross.'"[10]

Even though Jesus initially pushed back, He did perform His first miracle, or sign, as John called it. This act has less application in debates about alcoholic beverages and more to teach us about Jesus's identity. He revealed His glory.

What stands out to you as significant in this passage?

You may have written any number of things, but I noticed that Jesus's first miracle was high in quantity and quality. Each of the six stone jars filled with water for ritual cleansing held twenty to thirty gallons. So Jesus made up to 180 gallons of wine. Most commentators agree that "this large amount is a sign of the abundance of God's grace."[11] To use the stone jars for wine would have violated custom, but Jesus valued people over customs. Also note that Jesus replaced Old Testament law (water for ceremonial cleansing) with abundant grace (high quality wine) ultimately pictured in the communion supper where wine represents His blood.

Jesus brought fullness where there was emptiness and joy where there was disappointment. He longs to do that in our lives as well.

Does emptiness and disappointment describe your current circumstances? If so, explain.

The first step to discovering the fullness and joy evidenced in Jesus's first sign is to do what He says. Obedience places us on the path to God's peace.

Where has God's Word been nudging you toward obedience? Make a few notes below.

John established Jesus's divinity in the beginning of this Gospel and now shows us His glory. Jesus's disciples believed in Him. We can choose to do the same. If we want God's peace, then we must live according to His plan.

Moses's first miracle turned water into blood, which was a plague of judgment. Jesus's first miracle turned water into wine, which was a blessing of grace.

Moses's final plague was the death of firstborn sons. Jesus's final sign in John's Gospel is the raising of Lazarus.

The Synoptic Gospels (Matthew, Mark, Luke) placed the cleansing of the temple much closer to Jesus's death chronologically, whereas John set it at the beginning of His ministry. Scholars suggest that either Jesus cleared the temple twice or, in the practice of ancient biography, John rearranged the sequence to clarify his teaching point.[12]

THE PASSION

Once Jesus began His ministry, He traveled from Galilee to Jerusalem to celebrate the Passover with His disciples. There He continued to reveal Himself as the Son of God.

READ JOHN 2:13-22 and record the order of Jesus's actions (1 through 6):

___ **Poured out (or scattered) coins on the floor**

___ **Made a whip (or scourge)**

___ **Drove out everyone with sheep and cattle**

___ **Turned over tables**

___ **Told them to stop turning His Father's House into a marketplace (or house of trade, business, merchandise, market)**

___ **Chased out money changers**

What statement was Jesus making with His actions in the temple courts?

Jesus offers us abundant grace but desires His people to follow the Father's plan. In Jesus's day, that didn't include using the temple for profit. The condition of the temple was a vivid indication of the spiritual condition of the nation. The people were manipulating religion for money. Jesus knew there was no peace to be found in that practice, then or now.

He spoke boldly about abuses. The religious leaders asked for a sign. Jesus responded with prophetic words about destroying the temple and rebuilding it in three days. This confounded the leaders because Herod's temple, which was started in 20 BC, was not completed at the time of this encounter. However, Jesus wasn't talking about a building but His body. This kind of misunderstanding of spiritual truth, where hearers misinterpreted Jesus's words, is found throughout John's Gospel.[13]

Jesus is full of grace but also full of truth. Peace in following Him is not always found in the path of least resistance. Sometimes doing what He says means doing hard things.

STOP AND SAVOR

Today we focused on this truth: *If we desire the peace of Jesus, then we must do what He says.*

What's one thing you hope to remember about what you studied today?

What stood out to you from Jesus's words and actions?

How have you noticed a connection between obedience and peace in your life?

Jesus, I long to do what you say. I understand that peace is found in obedience to you. Empower me through your grace to obey. In Jesus's name, Amen.

Day Four
YOU MUST BE BORN AGAIN

SCRIPTURE
FOCUS

John 2:23—3:21

BIG IDEA

Jesus makes a distinction between sincere and superficial belief.

The Greek word translated "believed" or "trusted" is pisteuo, which means "to think to be true, to be persuaded of, to credit, place confidence in."[14] We will encounter this word eighty-five times in the book of John.[15]

SINCERE BELIEF

In our study of John today, Jesus will discuss the process of spiritual birth with a seeker.

> **READ JOHN 2:23-25** to set the stage for that conversation. Describe what you discover about Jesus.

Our English translations sometimes miss the play on words used in the original Greek. In John 2:23, Jesus essentially said some people believed in Him, but He didn't believe in them. What we discover in this passage is that belief can be superficial. Jesus knew those who had sincere belief and those just momentarily awed by miracles.

Signs could be the place where faith starts. John recorded miracles in his Gospel for that purpose (John 20:30-31). But genuine belief was necessary for spiritual rebirth. Attractional activities that point to the gospel message aren't bad, they just aren't enough. A person must move from superficial to sincere belief. Jesus revealed in these verses that people who want to experience His works without submitting to His Word will not share His life.

BORN AGAIN

One man who saw Jesus's miraculous signs wasn't easily convinced; he asked questions to delve deeper into Jesus's teaching.

READ JOHN 3:1-12 and record the questions Nicodemus asked.

VERSE 4	VERSE 9

Nicodemus belonged to a group called the Pharisees whose focus was strict obedience to the law. He was also one of the seventy-one members of the Sanhedrin. Nicodemus approached Jesus using the term of respect —*Rabbi*—assuming Jesus was a teacher who came from God. What he didn't realize was that He was God who had come to teach!

Scholars have debated why Nicodemus came to Jesus at night. What might be a possible reason?

The Sanhedrin functioned as a Jewish governing body who made laws and enforced them. Imagine the supreme court and senate rolled into one.

Since the text doesn't tell us, we can only speculate.

- *Perhaps he feared what colleagues might think of him and didn't want to be seen with Jesus.*

- *Maybe he wanted undisturbed time with Jesus away from the crowd.*

- *As one with ruling authority, he might have been busy during the day with pressing responsibilities.*

Regardless of the reason for this encounter, we can find an application for our own lives. Public worship and study gatherings are important, but there are things we can't get from Jesus with the crowd. We need personal, intimate meetings with our Savior.

What spiritual rhythms have you put into place for your alone time with Jesus?

How do you think your life would be different if you had more personal time with the Lord each day?

Nicodemus acknowledged the signs Jesus performed but struggled with Jesus's teaching regarding spiritual rebirth. He couldn't move what Jesus was saying out of the realm of physical birth: "How can an old man go back into his mother's womb and be born again?" (v. 4). But Jesus stated this was a different kind of birth, one "of water and the Spirit" (v. 5).

What do you think He meant by water and Spirit?

Scholars do not agree on the exact meaning of Jesus's statement regarding water and Spirit. Some have latched onto this statement to assert baptism as a requirement for salvation. Water baptism is an important step of obedience for a Christian, but Jesus wasn't referencing it directly in this conversation. Some say both elements, water and spirit, point to a picture of life and together they refer to spiritual birth. Others say being "born of water" references physical birth, as during childbirth, a mother's amniotic sac breaks, releasing a watery substance. I lean toward this interpretation. So, Jesus was saying a person can't enter the kingdom of God without being born physically (water) and spiritually (Spirit).

Using the birth analogy, Jesus revealed that just as you cannot manufacture babies, you cannot manufacture Christians.[16] Yes, spiritual birth is a mystery, but it is necessary and observable. Jesus used the wind to illustrate. You don't know the origin of the wind, but its effects are evident. In the same way, spiritual birth can't be seen, but the transformation is unmistakable.

If you have experienced spiritual birth as Jesus described, what's been the effect on your life?

Spiritual birth occurs at the moment of sincere belief. I believed in Jesus when I was nine years old. The transformation wasn't hugely evident in the following days and months, but over the course of forty years God's Spirit has changed everything.

LIFTED UP

READ JOHN 3:13-21 and record below the benefits associated with belief in these verses.

VERSE 15	VERSE 16	VERSE 18

Those who believe in Jesus ("the Son") receive eternal life and have no judgment against them, because Jesus came not to condemn but to save. This is good news!

Jesus foreshadowed how salvation would be accomplished with an Old Testament reference. In Numbers 21:4-9, the Lord sent poisonous snakes among the people of Israel because of their complaining. Many people were bitten and died. When Moses interceded for the people, God instructed him to make a bronze replica of a snake and attach it to a pole. The people were to look at it to be healed.

As the snake replica was lifted up on a pole and the Israelites found healing, Jesus would be lifted up on a cross so we could, by faith, find salvation in Him. As pastor R.C. Sproul said, "It is the good news that snake-bitten people, people infected by a poison that goes to the depth of their souls, can look to the cross and find salvation."[19]

Jesus made a play on words in the Greek. Wind is pneuma in Greek, which "can mean wind, breath, or spirit. He said, 'you have to be born of the Spirit, and it's like the wind.' In other words, the pneuma is like the pneuma."[17]

"Lifting up" is a term used in Scripture for both "exaltation and execution."[18]

Jesus used several illustrations to help explain salvation—birth, wind, the serpent on a pole, light and darkness. Which is the most helpful to you in wrapping your mind around what it means to be a Christian?

God loved us so much He sent Jesus to save us from sin. Yet we must believe in Him. This belief must move beyond a superficial longing for His works to a sincere faith that trusts His Word.

STOP AND SAVOR

Today we focused on this truth: *Jesus makes a distinction between sincere and superficial belief.*

What's one thing you hope to remember about what you studied today?

What stood out to you about what Jesus said?

Meditate for a moment about eternal life—living forever with Jesus. Savor this gift as it relates to your past, present, and future.

Day Five
HE MUST INCREASE

READ JOHN 3:22-30 and circle the letter that best answers the following questions:

What were both Jesus and John the Baptist doing?

    A. Sleeping

    B. Baptizing

    C. Healing

What did John the Baptist's disciples complain about?

    A. The Jew who debated with them over ceremonial cleansing

    B. The temperature of the baptismal waters

    C. People leaving their ministry for another

How did John the Baptist respond to their complaints?

    A. No one receives anything unless God gives it.

    B. I have told you plainly, I am not the Messiah.

    C. Jesus must increase, and I must decrease.

    D. All of the above.

How did John the Baptist see himself according to these verses?

How did he see Jesus?

SCRIPTURE FOCUS

John 3:22–36

BIG IDEA

More of God, less of me.

John the Baptist gave an honest assessment. He didn't discount his ministry or purpose; he leaned into his high calling from God to prepare the way for Jesus. For a season this meant greater visibility and recognition. However, he trusted God's plan—realizing the time had come for a decrease in his baptisms, preaching, and popularity.

What does it mean for Christ to increase and you to decrease? Where does this need to happen in your life?

KEEP JESUS AT THE CENTER

Scholars are uncertain who is speaking the words in verses 31-36. It could be Jesus, John the Gospel writer, or John the Baptist. I tend to see this as John the Baptist.

READ JOHN 3:31-35 and record below any words or phrases used to describe Jesus.

Rather than strategize enticing ways to win back the crowd, John the Baptist made Jesus the focus of discussion. His heart was for his followers to be followers of Jesus. John the Baptist highlighted the eternal plan above earthly priorities.

When I'm talking to others, I want to keep Jesus at the center to help them see beyond their current circumstances, but there's tension here. How do I listen to people's concerns, validate their feelings, yet at the same time point them toward God without seeming preachy or hyper-spiritual?

What are practical ways you have directed a conversation toward God in these situations?

John's mention of the Holy Spirit in verse 34 reminds me that inviting the Spirit to guide us is another practical way to seek God over self.

> **How would our lives change if we talked to God first when problems arise in our schools, friendships, families, and churches?**

Sincere belief in God's Son connects us to the Father. Jesus is the plan. We can savor peace when we savor Jesus.

STOP AND SAVOR

Today we focused on this truth: *More of God, less of me.*

> **What's one thing you hope to remember about what you studied today?**

> **What qualities of Jesus stood out to you in today's verses?**

> **What do you need to apply from John the Baptist's testimony and teaching?**

PRAYER

Jesus, help me to see myself clearly so that I can see you clearly. You must increase and I must decrease. This is so counter-intuitive to what my flesh and the world tell me about myself. Help me to lift others up toward you rather than be dragged down. Renew my mind with your truth so that I can find peace in your plan for me. In Jesus's name, Amen.

BEGIN

If you could plan a dream day, what would it look like?

Circle the emotion that best describes how you feel about your time with God this week. Share your answer with the group.

Happy   Content   Anxious   Sad   Angry

If you could use any color to describe how you feel about life in general right now, what would it be? Why?

Review the big ideas from this session. Which one did you enjoy the most? If any, which one did you struggle to relate to?

Based on your study from John 1–3, what are two qualities of Jesus that stand out to you?

As a group, review your memory verse from this session (John 1:12).

Choose one person to pray over the group and for your discussion time, that it would be beneficial for everyone and honoring to God.

REVIEW & DISCUSS

Share about a time when a plan fell through. Describe how you felt and your initial response.

Using the scale below, how would you describe your trust in God's plans?

Not at all.   Sometimes, I prefer my way.   Full surrender to Him.

READ JOHN 1:1-5. Do you know where the other verse in the Bible with the words "in the beginning" is found? (Hint: Go to the beginning!)

What (or WHO) does this verse say was there at the beginning?

If the Word was there at the beginning, circle what must be true:

  A. Jesus is also God.

  B. Jesus was part of God's plan from the beginning.

  C. Jesus didn't just prepare the way for salvation. He was the way.

  D. All of the above.

READ JOHN 1:14-18,29. How did John the Baptist describe Jesus?

We couldn't save ourselves from our sin. We needed Jesus to come and sacrifice His life for us, so we could experience forgiveness and a relationship with Him. What questions do you still have about Jesus's gift of salvation?

REFLECT & APPLY

If we can trust God's plan to send Jesus as our savior, how does that make Him trustworthy with His plans for our lives?

How does knowing who God is help us when our plans don't work out, or if we don't like the plans that are unfolding?

Next to each time frame below, write one plan you need to trust God with in order to experience His peace:

☐ Today

☐ This Week

☐ This Year

Grab a note card, then write down this session's memory verse: John 5:24. Discuss one or two ways that will help you memorize this verse before the next group time.

✕ CLOSE

Give each person a note card to write a prayer request on, then collect them in a bowl. Let each person choose a card out of the bowl to specifically pray over in the week ahead.

Before Next Time

HERE'S WHAT YOU'LL BE WORKING ON:
- Watch Session 3 Video
- Complete Session 3 Personal Study Days (as best you can!)
- Memorize John 5:24
- Stop and Savor

13

Peace in the Power of Jesus

I tell you the truth,
those who listen to my message
and believe in God who sent me
have eternal life. They will never be
condemned for their sins, but they
have already passed from death
into life.

John 5:24

Day One
POWER TO KNOW

SCRIPTURE
FOCUS

John 4:1–42

BIG IDEA

Peace is a Person.

"Pious Jews usually traveled around Samaria to avoid defilement, but for Jesus defilement came from within, not from without, and thus he took the shortest route, which was along the top of the ridge that passed by Sychar and Jacob's well."[1]

Peace isn't something we create or conjure. It's a gift we receive through close relationship with the Prince of Peace. We need to hold onto this important truth as we continue to savor peace in a chaotic world through John's Gospel. Today we travel to the village of Sychar in Samaria where Jesus first revealed Himself as the Messiah. He unveiled His identity to a woman who became perhaps the first gospel evangelist.

A JEWISH MAN

READ JOHN 4:1-9 and identify the two barriers that caused the woman to be surprised by Jesus's request for a drink.

Jesus's request crossed gender and racial lines. The text indicates that Jesus was sitting beside the well and didn't move when the woman arrived. This was not the usual practice. As scholar Kenneth Bailey states: "On seeing her, Jesus was expected to courteously withdraw to a distance of at least twenty feet, indicating that it was both safe and culturally appropriate to approach the well."[2] Not only did Jesus stay put, He also spoke to her. To help us wrap our minds around how outlandish this would have been at the time, Bailey adds this insight: "In village society, a strange man does not even make eye contact with a woman in a public place."[3]

Jesus's request for water was not only directed toward a woman, but a Samaritan woman. In doing so, Jesus ignored more than five hundred years of hostility between Jews and Samaritans. When Assyria conquered the Northern Kingdom of Israel in 722 BC, they exported most of the Jews back to Assyria. They then repopulated the area with pagan people, who intermarried with the remaining Jews. This created a mixed-race people who pure-blood Jews viewed as ethnically and religiously corrupted. Thus the animosity. But Jesus set it all aside and asked her for a drink.

Jesus approached this Samaritan woman from a place of need. He elevated her worth by looking at her, speaking to her, and asking something from her.

What does Jesus's encounter with the woman of Samaria say about Him?

A RABBI

READ JOHN 4:10-18 and note what Jesus revealed about Himself in these verses.

Village women in Jesus's day usually went to a well early in the morning or just before sundown to avoid the heat of the day. They traveled in groups for propriety's sake and to help each other lift the heavy jars.[4]

Perhaps you wrote "gift from God" or "living water" or noted Jesus's ability to know the woman's marital history. But this nameless woman was thinking in terms of physical, tangible realities. She questioned His lack of bucket and rope. She wanted His water if it made her life easier. She was thinking only of temporal gifts from God.

She was focused on water to sustain physical life, while Jesus was pointing her to Living Water to provide eternal life. Jesus is the *Logos*—the Living Word who offers Living Water to us.

Journal below what thoughts or questions come to mind as you think about Jesus's offer of Living Water.

A PROPHET

READ JOHN 4:19-24 and briefly explain the new issue the woman brought to Jesus now that she saw Him as a prophet.

The Samaritan woman's history had been exposed, but she didn't want to discuss those details. She wanted to talk about the correct place of worship. Jesus took the opportunity to clarify true worship.

What did He reveal in John 4:24?

Jesus wanted her to understand that God can't be confined to one location or defined in terms of a material being. Worship of Him isn't limited to a place or race. His character is infinitely beyond our limited views but intimately more personal than we could ever imagine.

The Samaritan woman focused on worship logistics, while Jesus brought it back to the heart.

How do we lose sight of what true worship of God is about?

THE MESSIAH

READ JOHN 4:25-42 and answer the following questions:

What did Jesus reveal to the woman in verse 26?

How did the woman respond to Jesus revealing Himself as Messiah?

What ultimately resulted from Jesus's conversation with the woman at the well (vv. 39-42)?

The woman experienced the spring of Living Water that Jesus referenced. She told everyone, "Come and see a man who told me everything I ever did!" (v. 29a). This was a sensational but effective advertisement because the people in the village knew her history. The text informs us that when she ran back to the village, she left her water bucket behind. She had come seeking well water but left carrying the promise of divine water.

Today's account reminds us that Jesus came to be our peace. He knows us fully—all our messy history—yet still came to earth to die for our sins. We might look for momentary peace from Amazon®, social media, a relationship, or a different church, but ultimately, peace is a Person, and His name is Jesus.

STOP AND SAVOR

Today we focused on this truth: *Peace is a Person.*

What's one thing you hope to remember about what you studied today?

What of Jesus's words and actions in this story stick out to you? Why?

How comforting and encouraging is it to know peace is not just a concept but a Person?

Day Two

POWER TO HEAL

SCRIPTURE FOCUS

John 4:43—5:15

BIG IDEA

In order to savor Jesus, we must stop limiting His ability to heal.

Have you ever gotten frustrated when a friend or sibling did something differently than you? For too many years, I attempted to conform my husband into being a studious planner like me. Though attracted to Sean's spontaneity and wonder, I often tried to change him to be more serious and practical.

As I began to recognize my tendencies, I was able to appreciate Sean for the unique way God made him and see how he is a good balance for me. Becoming self-aware helped me realize my wiring caused me to view Sean through a lens of unfair expectations. Just as our filters affect the way we see other people, they can also impact our understanding of God.

REQUIRING REACTION

READ JOHN 4:43-54 and answer the following questions:

What event does John remind us of that had previously happened in Cana? Why do you think this information is included in the text?

Who approached Jesus and what was his request?

How did Jesus respond?

Capernaum to Cana was about twenty-five miles via a road that climbs approximately 1,350 feet.[5] Being willing to make such a difficult journey helps us understand the desperation that prompted the man to beg Jesus to come.

What was the conclusion of this encounter?

The official underestimated Jesus's power. Jesus didn't need to be present to heal. Ultimately, the man believed without a sign. And what started with a crisis belief later became a confirmed belief when he heard the timing of his son's recovery. This man's faith became contagious as his whole household ended up believing in Jesus.

Many during that time craved amazement. They wanted a Savior who would heal them, lift them from poverty, and end their oppression. But Jesus called them to dedication by revealing Himself throughout this Gospel as much more than a circumstantial fix. He was the Savior to be trusted with the outcomes in our lives.

What is one thing you are asking God for today?

What could a next step of faith look like as you trust God with His answer?

To savor peace in this chaotic world where family members get sick and disappointments abound, we need Scripture to shape our understanding of Jesus, His purposes, and His ways. We can ask God for anything in prayer, but we cannot limit Him to our parameters.

RELIGIOUS SUPERSTITION

READ JOHN 5:1-9a and either draw or briefly describe the scene below.

The lame man Jesus encountered at the pool had bought into a superstition about the waters' healing powers. Evidently something (perhaps a spring) caused the waters to periodically stir. When the disturbance occurred, people believed the first person in the water would be healed. The lame man's belief was rooted in mysticism, which seems incongruent with Judaism. Yet it was common for people "to believe in magic alongside institutional religion."[6]

What two inhibitors to healing did the lame man mention in verse 7?

He blamed his lack of help and others being faster than him getting into the waters. Yet he missed the significance of the question about true wellness because he could only process within the framework of his current reality and capabilities. However, Jesus didn't rebuke his limited understanding but instead expanded it with three commands.

What did Jesus tell the man to do in verse 8?

What needs healing in your life? It could be a relationship, physical body, mind, spiritual health, and so forth.

What excuses for not experiencing healing come to mind as you consider becoming whole in this area?

Write a prayer below and ask Jesus to perform a healing work in your life today.

Healing is a difficult topic. The poolside portico was filled with lame, paralyzed, and sick people, but Jesus approached only one man. Then, after the healing, Jesus "disappeared into the crowd" (John 5:13). (The Greek word for "there" means "to dodge."[7]) We don't know Jesus's motives regarding this biblical situation or His response to situations that happen in our lives. I've been asked questions like these:

- Why did God heal my grandma's cancer only to allow it to return?
- Why are my friends' parents happily married while mine are divorced?
- Why did their anxiety go away while mine persists?

I'm sure you could add other difficult questions that don't have easy answers. Sometimes, the best we can do is acknowledge God's power to heal and accept His decisions regarding how and when it occurs. On the days it feels like we are ones who were dodged, may we find peace in God's sovereignty and presence.

RULES OVER RELATIONSHIP

READ JOHN 5:9b-16 and briefly explain what upset the Jewish leaders.

when John talked about "the Jews" or "the Jewish leaders" he was not making a racial or ethnic designation. He used that phrase to describe Jesus's religious opponents.[8]

Jesus didn't heal on the Sabbath by accident. He knew the regulations about work on the Sabbath that had been added to the law. Perhaps He chose the day of rest to upset the religious leaders and bring the issue to the front. It's hard to wrap our minds around the religious leaders' focus on minutia in the midst of a miracle. Their lives revolved around the law. And while the law was good, even good things can lead to spiritual blindness.

Today, we saw three people with three different blind spots that caused them to limit God's power:

1. The government official was laser focused on his immediate need and limited God's power to a location.

2. The lame man blended mysticism with his religious beliefs and limited God to a magical pool.

3. The Jewish leaders elevated rules over relationships and limited when God's healing power could be expressed.

What limits have you projected on God? Is there something you think He can't or won't do? Share about it in the space below.

Jesus, help me to see you clearly. Reveal any blind spots that might be filtering my view of you. I want to know you and savor your peace in my life today. Thank you for ultimate healing through your blood shed on the cross. In Jesus's name, Amen.

Are there any blind spots (past experiences, your exposure to social media, your friend group) that are causing you to limit God? If so, what are they?

How can you get rid of those blind spots and limitations in order to fully trust God's ability to work in your life?

STOP AND SAVOR

Today we focused on this truth: *In order to savor Jesus, we must stop limiting His ability to heal.*

What's one thing you hope to remember about what you studied today?

What stood out to you about what Jesus said and did?

How can you savor the peace of Jesus even when His actions and timing don't fulfill your requests?

Day Three
THE SOURCE OF POWER

Our focus this week is on savoring peace in the power of Jesus. We've seen Jesus's power on display in His interaction with the Samaritan woman and in healing the government official's son and the paralyzed man by the pool in Bethesda. Yet He faced opposition from Jewish leaders for displaying that power on the Sabbath.

When the leaders challenged Jesus, He responded by explaining His identity in relation to the Father. Jesus revealed Himself as the Son of God sent by God—and God Himself.

SCRIPTURE FOCUS

John 5:16–45

BIG IDEA

We can savor peace by finding our power and identity in the Son of God.

HIS IDENTITY

READ JOHN 5:16-23 and record what you learn about the Father and the Son in the chart below:

FATHER	SON
Verse 17	Verse 17
Verse 20	Verse 19
Verse 21	Verse 21
Verse 22	Verse 22

What stands out to you about the Father/Son relationship described by Jesus in these verses?

This passage shows the unity between the Father and the Son. They are both always working. And as the Father gives life, Jesus is entrusted with the authority to both give life and to judge. While the Son was not sent to condemn the world (John 3:17), He has the authority to judge those who choose unbelief.

Jesus knew His source of power and identity was in the Father. We find our identity in the Son and live by the power of His Holy Spirit. When we face criticism, knowing whose we are provides peace worth savoring. This passage not only teaches important Christology (the study of Christ) but also provides a model for us in times of opposition.

OUR IDENTITY

Write John 5:24 (our memory verse this week) below.

According to John 5:24, what do you know for sure about yourself today?

Here we find rich truth that can give us confidence. By faith in God through Christ we have passed from death to life and are no longer condemned. We are forever secure in Him. So when we face opposition or feel attacked—at work, in a relationship, or online—let's remember whose we are. Better yet, when our spiritual enemy accuses us, we don't have to listen to him. We stand in the truth of who we are in Christ. We're still going to make mistakes, mess up relationships and apologize, seek counsel in decisions, and need to change our behavior. But we always have hope in Him. Jesus said He could do nothing on His own, and neither can we. Instead, we rely on His power and who He says we are to shape our identity and confidence.

ALREADY AND NOT YET

READ JOHN 5:25-30 and record references to timing of important events in these verses:

Verse 25

Verses 28-29

Jesus said there is a time coming and is here now when the dead will hear His voice and those who listen will receive life (v. 25). This speaks to the ministry of Jesus, then and now, as the life-giver. There is present opportunity for salvation. However, there's a future time coming when all the dead will be raised, some to eternal life, some to judgment. This concept of already and not yet regarding God's kingdom can be difficult to wrap our minds around. However, Jesus used a phrase to describe Himself that would have helped the original audience to understand His meaning. It came from a prophecy in Daniel 7:13-14.

READ THAT PASSAGE below and underline the same phrases as found in John 5:27:

As my vision continued that night, I saw someone like a son of man coming with the clouds of heaven. He approached the Ancient One and was led into his presence. He was given authority, honor, and sovereignty over all the nations of the world, so that people of every race and nation and language would obey him. His rule is eternal—it will never end. His kingdom will never be destroyed.
DANIEL 7:13-14

Eschatology is "a branch of theology concerned with the final events in the history of the world or of humankind."[9]

With His use of "Son of Man," the Jews would likely have made the connection to Daniel's writing immediately and realized that Jesus was claiming to be both the Messiah and the Judge.[10] Passages like this one also give us reason to trust our Father with future events. The apostle Paul reminded us that right now we see only in part but one day God will make everything clear (1 Cor. 13:12). For now we accept that Christ has already come, and He has not yet returned.

WITNESSES

READ JOHN 5:31-47. In this passage Jesus identified four witnesses who demonstrated His claim. Draw a line to match the reference with the witness.

Verses 32–35 — Jesus's teaching and miracles

Verse 36 — The Father

Verses 37–38 — The Scriptures

Verse 39 — John the Baptist

Witness is used forty-seven times in John's Gospel.[11]

When people got Jesus wrong, they got God wrong. Though the religious leaders knew the words of God, they did not know the Word of God (John 1:1,11), thus they did not know God Himself. As we think about what we look to for our own power and identity, we need a moment of self-reflection. Are we trusting in our knowledge, education, position, or experience more than Christ? Pastor Warren Wiersbe put it this way, "Does our knowledge of the Bible give us a 'big head' or a 'burning heart'?"[12] I'm not in any way discouraging us from reading and studying Scripture, for when we do so rightly, it always leads us to Jesus—to know Him better and become more like Him. It's just that we must do so with the right intention of the heart.

Jesus clearly showed Himself to be the Son of God who gives life and renders judgment but does nothing by Himself. The religious leaders of His day missed this truth. Let's make sure this doesn't happen to us.

STOP AND SAVOR

Today we focused on this truth: *We can savor peace by finding our power and identity in the Son of God.*

What's one thing you hope to remember about what you studied today?

What stood out to you about what Jesus said?

What attitude adjustments or action steps might the Holy Spirit be leading you to take in light of your study?

PRAYER

Jesus, thank you for being clear about your identity. I believe you are the Son of God. you are always working, your power comes from the Father, and you hold life and judgment in your capable hands. Help me to know and better understand who you are and who I am in you through John's Gospel. In Jesus's name, Amen.

Day Four
MIRACULOUS POWER

SCRIPTURE FOCUS

John 6:1–21

BIG IDEA

We can savor peace by embracing Jesus for who He revealed Himself to be rather than who we want Him to be.

The feeding of the multitudes:

- *Matthew 14:13–21*
- *Mark 6:31–44*
- *Luke 9:12–17*
- *John 6:1–14*

Jesus walking on water:

- *Matthew 14:22–34*
- *Mark 6:45–53*
- *John 6:15–21*

At a conference I attended, one of the speakers showed a series of images of Jesus commonly found on church walls. The first was smiling, playful Jesus—one with Him having fun with the children. Next the speaker showed good buddy Jesus—cool, friendly Jesus from an animated series. The third image was spooky Jesus—an expressionless face with a weird light glowing above Him. Finally, for humor, he showed a picture he referred to as bearded lady Jesus—a feminine looking face with a beard. His point was that each artist rendered Jesus from a personal point of view.

If you've seen drawings of Jesus, describe the background/ setting and what He looked like in those pictures.

Today, in John 6, we are going to find two stories of Jesus's miraculous power: the feeding of the multitudes and Jesus walking on water. The first is the only miracle (except for the resurrection) recorded in all four Gospels, and the second is recorded in every Gospel except Luke's. Our takeaway from these incredible displays will not be about sharing our food, the need to clean up leftovers, or remembering to bring extra life jackets on boat rides. Instead, we will see how these events clarify our theology regarding Jesus. In order to accomplish this, we will continually ask this question: Who is Jesus? We will lay aside mental pictures from the past and ask the Lord to reveal Himself anew to us through His Word.

Normally, we pray at the end of each day's study, but before you open the text today, pray something like this:

Jesus, I want to know You. I long to experience Your power. Please check my motives that I might desire just You—not what You can do to fix my current problems or so that I can feel better about myself. Help me to see You clearly so I can love You with my whole heart. Use Your Word to shape my view of You—the Living Word. In Jesus's name, Amen.

THE NOTICER

READ JOHN 6:1-5 and answer the following questions:

Why was the crowd following Jesus?

What holy day did this event precede?

What question did Jesus ask Phillip and why did He ask it?

Verse 5 says Jesus "saw a huge crowd of people," which seems like an insignificant detail. However, the Greek expression used here literally says Jesus "lifted up His eyes." It gives us an answer to our question, *Who is Jesus?* He noticed the people and had compassion for their physical needs. Jesus is the Son of God who lifts His eyes to notice what is happening in our world.

Jesus is God, and yet He notices you. As Jesus lifts His eyes in your direction today, what does He notice about your needs?

THE TEACHER

READ JOHN 6:6-9. List the two disciples involved and a summary of their thoughts on the problem of hungry people:

VERSE(S)	DISCIPLE	SUMMARY
Verse 7		
Verses 8-9		

When Jesus asked Phillip the question about a place to buy food, we can almost hear Phillip doing mental arithmetic. He considered the amount of people to feed, then calculated the time and work needed to get that kind of money, and came up empty. However, he left Jesus completely out of his equations.

As did Andrew. He reported on the presence of a boy's lunch but knew the scarce amount would not be enough. But Jesus wants to teach us to think bigger. With Him, nothing is impossible. Even the big problems become an opportunity to get closer to Him.

When you think about the big problems in your life, what should your response be?

Panic / Freak out   Take Control Myself   Trust God Fully

THE GENEROUS HOST

READ JOHN 6:10-11 and number Jesus's actions in the order they appear in the verses from 1 to 5:

_____ He took the loaves.

_____ He distributed the fish.

_____ He gave thanks to God.

_____ He distributed the bread.

_____ He told everyone to sit down.

Jesus supernaturally provided. Although the crowd came for healing, Jesus was a generous host who fed them. Reading accounts like this one realigns my thinking. So often I live with a scarcity mentality—as if God is limited.

Are there circumstances in your life where you've limited God's power or ability to intervene? Explain.

THE GATHERER

READ JOHN 6:12-13. Why did Jesus say to gather up the leftovers?

Philip, being from nearby Bethsaida, likely knew best how to obtain food in that area (John 1:44).[13]

Jesus said nothing was to be wasted. He won't waste anything in your life either—your pain, your leftover fragments of a broken relationship, your consequences from poor choices. He will use it for your good and His glory.

THE PROPHET AND KING

READ JOHN 6:14-15 and answer the following questions:

Who did the people decide Jesus was?

The five thousand represents men, so the actual number of people, including women and children, could have been significantly more than ten thousand.[14]

What did they want to do about it?

What did Jesus do in response?

Jesus was a Prophet and King but not in the sense the people wanted Him to be. They tried to force Him into their portrait of a warrior king with an earthly kingdom who would release them from political oppression. They couldn't reconcile how they wanted Him to act with how He acted. But Jesus the Prophet came as a Suffering Servant—to do God's will, not the people's will.

How have you seen people (media, people in your sphere) twist their understanding of Jesus to fit their mold?

It's well
documented
that the Sea of
Galilee is prone
to sudden storms.
That's what likely
occurred in the
John 6 story of
Jesus walking on
the water.[15]

THE WATER WALKER

READ JOHN 6:16-21. What did Jesus call out to the men in the boat (v. 20)?

This story provides an interlude before Jesus connects the feeding of the crowd with His identity as the Bread of Life. It puzzles me that the disciples witnessed an incredible miracle, then only hours later a storm scared them. Yet, isn't that us? We see God work and our trust grows. But then the next storm frightens us. Jesus provides for us and calms our storms. He is the Creator who is in control of His creation. He is present with you.

Where is He calling you to release fear and savor His peace today? Reflect and journal some notes below.

We don't want to create an inaccurate picture of Jesus shaped by our feelings, personality, or what culture says about Him. We don't need a spooky Jesus or a buddy Jesus, we need the real Jesus.

STOP AND SAVOR

Today we focused on this truth: *We can savor peace by embracing Jesus for who He revealed Himself to be rather than who we want Him to be.*

What's one thing you hope to remember about what you studied today?

How can you lift up your eyes (from screens, tasks, distractions) and see Jesus more clearly today?

PRAYER

Jesus, thank you for being a powerful and attentive provider and rescuer. You are so gracious and generous. Forgive me for fashioning you into who I want you to be instead of embracing you for who you really are. You are my Lord and Savior. I love you and bow before you. In Jesus's name, Amen.

Day Five
EXCHANGED POWER

My best friend got a new puppy named Gemma. Gemma struggles with a misplaced appetite. She eats everything, including things that make her sick, like socks, balloons, and Wiffle® balls. While we chuckle at Gemma's strange obsession, sometimes it's not funny. Her stomach has been scanned more than once, and she has often lacked basic nutrition. She loves to eat but fills herself with objects that can't nourish her.

While we're not likely to eat socks, we also struggle with our appetites.

What's a food you've been craving lately?

I'm guessing most of us didn't write "salad" as our answers. We often desire food that brings instant pleasure but lacks needed nutrients. The food issues for Jesus's original audience looked a little different than ours. Most of them weren't trying to limit their food intake but rather working to ensure they had enough to survive.

Jesus had provided bread and fish for a huge crowd who now wanted more of that kind of miracle. But Jesus didn't come just to fill their stomachs. He cared for physical needs but longed for them to prioritize their spiritual hunger. Like this crowd, we can become overly focus on the urgent and miss the important.

SPENDING YOUR ENERGY

READ JOHN 6:22-29 and answer the following questions:

Why did Jesus say the people were seeking Him?

What did Jesus say the people should work for or spend their energy doing?

SCRIPTURE FOCUS

John 6:22–71

BIG IDEA

When we focus on fulfilling our physical appetites, we can miss the One who longs to satisfy our spiritual hunger.

What was their request, and how did Jesus reply in verses 28-29? What did Jesus mean?

The people couldn't lift their minds above the physical necessities of life. Jesus was not commanding them to stop working for a living or to stop eating real food. He would never shame anyone for needing food, but He knows the weakness that accompanies spiritual emptiness.

That emptiness or restlessness of our souls won't be fulfilled with any kind of accomplishment, social media binge, hobbies, or human relationships. Therefore, we must spend our energy on eternal pursuits such as prayer, God's Word, rest, godly community, and other spiritual practices that help us feast on the Bread of Life.

What would it look like for you to feed your spiritual appetite today?

The phrase "I tell you the truth" or "truly, truly I say unto you" (John 6:32,47,53) is the Greek word for "amen" repeated twice. Jesus used it for emphasis at the beginning of important revelations.

SEEING BEYOND

READ JOHN 6:30-59.

What smells, tastes, or images come to mind as you think about bread?

My husband makes bread in our electric bread maker. I can barely wait for it to cool before slathering it with butter or honey! It is definitely something to savor. In this passage, Jesus revealed Himself to be the source of spiritual nourishment. Yet the crowd just wanted what Jesus could give them, not Jesus Himself. They asked for more signs and referenced the manna God gave the Israelites as a temporary provision during their wilderness years (Ex. 16:14-15). They likely mentioned manna because of "a Jewish expectation that, when the Messiah came, He would renew the miracle of manna."[16] They wanted more evidence and more bread. Yet while they wanted Jesus's physical power to fix their earthly problems, Jesus offered spiritual power to savor His peace for all eternity.

STAYING THE COURSE

READ JOHN 6:60-71 and identify the responses of the following people:

Many of His disciples (v. 66)

Simon Peter (v. 68)

Jesus's true disciples stayed the course through miraculous signs and hard spiritual truths. Those who were superficially attracted to the sensational fell away. Superficial belief falters, but steadfast faith remains. We don't move to steadfast faith by trying harder because Jesus said that human effort accomplishes nothing. Instead, we need to eat the Bread of Life. We realize and proclaim as Peter did that our only hope is in Jesus. Only He has the words of life. So we trust Him, surrender, and follow.

STOP AND SAVOR

Today we focused on this truth: *When we focus only on fulfilling our physical appetites, we can miss the One who longs to satisfy our spiritual hunger.*

What's one thing you hope to remember about what you studied today?

What surprised you about Jesus's responses or questions?

The term "disciples" used in verse 66 is a blanket term referring to people who were following Jesus to learn from His messages. The Greek word for "disciple" simply means "learner."[17]

PRAYER

Jesus, help me to savor my relationship with you. I don't want to treat you like a vending machine—just looking for what I can get from your power. Instead, help me to spend my energy on eternal things, see beyond temporary circumstances, and stay the course in my relationship with you. Help me to savor peace in your power even when I can't see or feel it. I believe you are the Bread of Life! In Jesus's name, Amen.

BEGIN

If you could only eat one form of potato for the rest of your life, what would it be?

Circle the emotion that best describes how you feel about your time with God this week. Share your answer with the group.

Happy   Content   Anxious   Sad   Angry

If you could use any color to describe how you feel about life in general right now, what would it be? Why?

Review the big ideas from this session. Which one did you enjoy the most? If any, which one did you struggle to relate to?

Based on your study from John 4–6, what are two qualities of Jesus that stand out to you?

As a group, review your memory verse from this session (John 5:24).

Choose one person to pray over the group and for your discussion time, that it would be beneficial for everyone and honoring to God.

REVIEW & DISCUSS

Where is your favorite place you've ever traveled to? Describe the things you love about that place and explain why.

Did any of you say your favorite part was the entrance sign or the city marker that said you were close? Probably not, since signs aren't the main attraction. What is the purpose of signs?

Fill out the chart below to see three signs that Jesus gave to point people to Him.

	who?	what Happened?
John 4:46–50		
John 5:1–16		
John 6:1–16		

What were these signs supposed to point to?

READ JOHN 6:26. Why do you think they missed the point of Jesus's sign?

READ JOHN 6:35-36. While they wanted actual bread to eat, what was Jesus inviting them to?

REFLECT & APPLY

Often, we love what God can give us, but we don't appreciate who God is apart from what He can do for us. Why is that not okay?

Share a time when you have forgotten to savor your relationship with God apart from what He can do for you.

What does it look like in your day-to-day life to be satisfied in Jesus?

How are you feeding on the Bread of Life this week? Write down two practical ways this can happen.

1.

2.

Spend a few minutes alone to reflect on your belief in God. Why do you follow Him? Is your belief in Him superficial and based on what He does? How have you missed Jesus at work in your life? Reflect in the space below.

Grab a note card, then write down this session's memory verse: John 7:24. Discuss one or two ways that will help you memorize this verse before the next group time.

✕ CLOSE

Share prayer requests with your group. Write a request and name at the top of the personal study pages for this week. As you open your book each day, this will prompt you to pray for these needs as you study.

Before Next Time

HERE'S WHAT YOU'LL BE WORKING ON:
- **Watch Session 4 Video**
- **Complete Session 4 Personal Study Days (as best you can!)**
- **Memorize John 7:24**

SESSION

4

Peace in the Patience of Jesus

Look beneath the surface
so you can judge correctly.

John 7:24

Day One
PATIENT WITH PEOPLE

SCRIPTURE
FOCUS

John 7:1–36

BIG IDEA

People may try to
rush us, but we
can savor peace
in God's timing.

Today we will discover Jesus's patience with His family, His critics, and the crowd. Each of these groups attempted to direct Jesus regarding where He went, when He went, and what He should say and do. Jesus was patient with them, and He is also patient with us.

What current situations in your life present an opportunity for patience?

People may try to rush us, but we can savor peace in God's timing.

PATIENT WITH FAMILY

READ JOHN 7:1-9 and answer the following questions:

What festival was being celebrated?

Why did Jesus's brothers urge Him to go to Judea?

What do you think was their motivation?

What was Jesus's response to His brother's mocking statements? What did He mean?

Rather than approach Jesus's miracles and messages with belief, or just curiosity, Jesus's brothers acted as self-appointed campaign managers goading Him to do His works in public with the Feast of Tabernacles being a prime-time opportunity. But they were ignorant of His purpose and didn't have His best interest at heart. Jesus wouldn't be rushed. He listened to the Father for instruction. He wasn't going to let His brothers pressure Him into proving Himself. His time had not yet come.

Jesus didn't deceive them by saying He wasn't going, then going later. Their timing and what they wanted Him to do was different than His timing and purpose. He would eventually go, but He could not celebrate as a normal participant at the Feast of Tabernacles because He was the fulfillment of it. John 1:14 revealed that Jesus "dwelt among us" (CSB). "Dwelt" is the Greek word *skenoo,* which means "to fix one's tabernacle."[2] Ironically, while the Jews were busy setting up their tabernacles, they didn't realize that the fulfillment of their ceremonies walked among them.[3]

While His brothers used rhetoric to provoke Him, Jesus didn't argue or rebuke them. He tried to explain in a way their limited understanding could bear. He knew they would eventually have their eyes opened to the truth and be counted among the church's leaders (Acts 1:14; 1 Cor. 9:5; Gal 1:19). But, at this point, Jesus simply said, "My time has not yet come" (John 7:8).

Patience with family can be challenging. Jesus exercised patience toward His earthly brothers when they taunted Him. With His power we can show patience toward our family members as well.

> **How do you need to show patience toward a close friend or family member this week? Write one or two practical ways you can make that happen.**

It takes time to develop and maintain patience in our relationships, especially with close family. Be persistent, and recognize that both you and your family members can benefit from practicing patience together.

In Jesus's day, if the powers that be in Judea were looking for you, it would be safer for you to stay in Galilee, and vice versa, since the two regions were under separate jurisdictions.[1]

John's emphasis on pace and timing in the ministry of Jesus is unique from the Synoptic Gospels of Matthew, Mark, and Luke.

PATIENT WITH THE CROWD

READ JOHN 7:10-24 and write verse 24 in your own words below.

The New Living Translation says, "Look beneath the surface so you can judge correctly." This was the heart of Jesus's message as He patiently attempted to help the crowd understand His identity.

Our lens for seeing Jesus as He really is can become clouded with the traditions in which we were raised, media messages regarding God, or our own misconceptions about Him. Yet, Jesus patiently calls us to see beneath the surface so that we can judge correctly.

Think about a current frustrating or challenging situation regarding people (anything from a small annoyance to a severed relationship).

What are the surface details of what happened?

What might the Lord want you to see beneath the surface as you consider the feelings involved, past history, and potential growth in the situation?

Let's dig deep so we don't miss the eternal work God wants to do in our lives.

PATIENT WITH CRITICS

READ JOHN 7:25-36 and summarize the reasons the following people groups rejected Jesus:

The local people of Jerusalem (v. 27)

Pharisees (vv. 31-32)

How did these two groups fail to look beneath the surface?

The stumbling block for the people of Jerusalem was bad theology. They assumed the Messiah would instantaneously appear rather than be born into a family. The Pharisees felt threatened by His popularity. I can't help but be amazed at Jesus's patience with both groups.

In verse 30 we find John repeating the phrase, "because his time had not yet come." God's sovereign plan unfolded according to His timetable. Jesus didn't allow people to rush Him—whether they were family, crowds, or critics. He followed God's plan one step at a time.

STOP AND SAVOR

Today we focused on this truth: *People may try to rush us, but we can savor peace in God's timing.*

What's one thing you hope to remember about what you studied today?

How was Jesus's patience displayed in today's passage?

PRAYER

Lord, you are so patient with me. Help me get a clear view of you to know you in your fullness as Messiah King. Show me where I am stuck on surface things that keep me from knowing you deeply. Draw my heart toward you today and give me patience with the people in my life. In Jesus's name, Amen.

Day Two
A PATIENT INVITATION

SCRIPTURE
FOCUS
John 7:37–52

BIG IDEA
We are all dying of spiritual thirst, and Jesus invites us to drink His Living Water.

Our family took a trip out west with friends and extended family several years ago. We saw incredible sights, including a beautiful waterfall at Yellowstone National Park. However, to get to this waterfall, we had to hike a few miles on a hot day in July. My husband, Sean, was carrying a small cooler containing water bottles for our immediate family. He wanted to linger at the Grand Prismatic Spring (a colorful hot spring) longer than the rest of the antsy group, so he decided to meet us later on the trail. Unfortunately, Sean thought he spotted us going a different direction, so we never met up. By the time we returned to the car, we were mildly dehydrated and out of sorts.

> **When was the last time you remember being thirsty and not having access to water?**

In today's text, we'll find Jesus looking beneath the surface of physical thirst to address our spiritual dryness. He invites us to drink His Living Water.

DYING OF THIRST

> **READ JOHN 7:37-38** and answer these questions:
> **On which day of the Festival of Tabernacles did this occur?**

> **Summarize Jesus's invitation, including who could respond and what they would receive.**

What did Jesus mean by "living water" (v. 38)?

Part of the week-long Feast of Tabernacles (Booths/Shelters) was a water ceremony in which the people followed a priest who carried water in a golden cup from the pool of Siloam to the temple. This was to remind the Jews of God's miraculous provision of water from the rock while their ancestors were in the wilderness.[4] This procession was repeated once each day and seven times on the last day of the celebration.

More than once God miraculously provided water for the Israelites wandering in the desert. God turned bitter water into drinking water (Ex. 15:22-27). Moses struck a rock and water poured out (Ex. 17:1-7). In the wilderness, water was a life-or-death situation.[5]

In today's passage, Jesus didn't issue a collective call to a water ritual, but invited His hearers to an individual response of faith that would result in "rivers of living water" (John 7:38), flowing from the believer's heart to provide perpetual satisfaction of spiritual thirst.

How have you experienced spiritual thirst, and how has Jesus quenched your thirst as Living Water?

The people were sincere in their celebration of the Festival of Tabernacles, but they were missing the One who fulfilled its meaning. Jesus didn't mandate their belief but rather invited them to consider His invitation. The Lord continues patiently inviting today rather than forcing Himself upon His creation.

THE PROMISE OF THE SPIRIT

READ JOHN'S EDITORIAL COMMENT IN JOHN 7:39 and record what you learn about the Holy Spirit.

John explained that the "rivers of living water" (v. 38) Jesus promised was the Holy Spirit. He would be given to everyone who believes, but not until after Jesus ascended, or "entered into his glory" (v. 39).

Pentecost marked the beginning of the apostles' public ministry and the spread of Christianity beyond its initial followers.

God's Spirit was involved in creation and present among God's people during Old Testament times—empowering certain people for specific tasks. After Christ ascended to heaven, the Spirit came powerfully at Pentecost (Acts 2), permanently living within every person who followed Jesus from then on.

How have you experienced the Holy Spirit working in your life?

If you haven't sensed Him at work or would like to see His guidance in your life grow, how can you be more aware and connected to God's Spirit who lives within you?

In our study of John, our focus is savoring the peace of Jesus in a chaotic world. Read the verses below and circle the fruit found in the subtitle of our Bible study:

But the Holy Spirit produces this kind of fruit
in our lives: love, joy, peace, patience, kindness, goodness,
faithfulness, gentleness, and self-control.
There is no law against these things!
GALATIANS 5:22-23

As we pursue the peace and patience of Jesus, we are reminded that we can't manufacture either on our own. We savor both through God's Spirit who lives in us.

DEBATING THE SOURCE

READ JOHN 7:40-53 and fill in the chart on the following page with the different responses to Jesus's invitation:

VERSE(S)	PERSON/ PEOPLE	RESPONSE REGARDING JESUS
Verses 40-44	The crowd	
Verses 45-46	Temple guards	
Verses 47-49	Pharisees	
Verses 50-51	Nicodemus	
Verse 52	Pharisees (part 2)	

Some of the people thought Jesus might be the prophet whom Moses spoke about in Deuteronomy 18:15. There are other references to this "Prophet" in John 1:21,25; 6:14.

Some of the crowd believed Jesus was the Prophet, and some said He was the Messiah. Others had inaccurate information about Jesus's birthplace. The religious leaders scoffed about Him. Jesus didn't grade Himself based on the varied responses to His invitation. Instead, He listened to the Father for His timing and message.

How do you compare the way people responded to Jesus then to how they respond to Him today?

This passage reminds me that it's much easier to label people than listen to the facts. When the religious leaders couldn't answer the arguments of the temple guards or Nicodemus, they attacked the speaker. They even used racial prejudice against Galileans, which "was common in antiquity."[6]

Many religious people in the crowd at the Feast of Tabernacles missed the peace of God because of their preconceived ideas and superficial understandings. We want to learn from them what not to do so that we can savor the peace of Jesus and drink the Living Water of His Spirit today.

STOP AND SAVOR

Today we focused on this truth: *We are all dying of spiritual thirst, and Jesus invites us to drink His Living Water.*

What's one thing you hope to remember about what you studied today?

What stood out to you about what Jesus said?

What did you notice about His patience?

Day Three
A PATIENT RESPONSE

I'm sitting at my laptop debating which story of personal failure to tell you. I can recall many times when I said the wrong thing, took a course of action contrary to God's Word, or misread a situation. Because I'm a Bible study author, people sometimes assume I'm a better person than I am. However, I know all too well my bent toward selfishness, laziness, excess, and pride. This awareness of sin is vital when it comes to repentance but can be a danger when it leads me to self-condemnation. Perhaps you can relate to beating yourself up over your sin rather than repenting of it.

> **Are there condemning thoughts rolling around in your mind lately? If so, write a few of them below.**

Negative self-talk leads us away from God. Rather than throw stones at ourselves for being sinful humans, we can savor peace in this truth: Jesus won't condemn you, so you can stop condemning yourself.

> **What immediately comes to mind you when you hear that truth? Do you believe it? Why or why not?**

Before we dig into today's passage to see Jesus's radical response toward sin, we need to discuss a controversy that surrounds these verses. Regarding John 8:1-11, you may see a note/footnote in your Bible that reads something like this: *The most ancient Greek manuscripts do not include John 7:53–8:11.* Without getting too deep into the weeds, let's dispel any confusion surrounding this notation. Translators of the Bible relied on a variety of early manuscripts to produce the Bible you are using today. Textual criticism is a science that evaluates thousands of surviving copies of the New Testament to determine credibility. The consensus of textual critics is that this account was not a part of the original Gospel of John but is probably an authentic story that is helpful for us to understand the purpose and work of Jesus.

A SETUP FOR A SAVIOR

READ JOHN 8:1-11 and write brief observations regarding these individuals/groups.

• **Jesus**

• **The crowd**

• **Scribes (teachers of religious law) and Pharisees**

• **The woman caught in adultery**

In Jesus's day, the temple area had large walkways throughout. At the north end, Herod the Great had built a military fort knowing that much civil unrest was connected with the temple. Roman officers patrolled the walkways looking for any signs of disturbance among the people, particularly during festivals.[8]

I'm wondering why the man caught in adultery wasn't mentioned. The experts in the law certainly knew that both participants were required to be put to death (Lev. 20:10; Deut. 22:22). Another question that comes to mind is how the religious leaders happened to catch this couple in the act. Several scholars speculate that perhaps the scribes and Pharisees set up this scenario in order to trap Jesus in a no-win situation.

The religious leaders didn't ask a hypothetical question. They put the accused woman right in front of Jesus. She became a prop in their plan to force Him to either break Roman law or disagree with Moses. The Romans denied the Jews the right to put anyone to death (John 18:31). So if Jesus initiated a stoning, nearby Roman soldiers would likely rush to the commotion and arrest Jesus. If Jesus disagreed with stoning, then it would discredit Him as contradicting the Law of Moses. The religious leaders wanted Him gone by any means necessary. They cared more about turf than truth.

How did Jesus handle what appeared to be a no-win situation? (Consider specifically His pace, His posture, and His words.)

Jesus was patient when cornered. He didn't use the tactics we saw employed in the previous chapter by the religious elite: attack the speaker (John 7:44-48), twist the truth (v. 49), and redirect with prejudice (v. 52). Jesus took His time, physically got low, and spoke few but compelling words. Whether we are the one caught in sin, part of the crowd drifting away, or having a Pharisee moment of manipulation, Jesus responds to us with grace and truth.

> **When you mess up, what picture do you have of Jesus in that moment?**

Fuming with Anger   *Rolling His eyes*   *Full of Grace & Truth*

A PATIENT RESPONSE

Some say Jesus wrote a list of the accusing men's specific sins.[10] Others surmise it could have been any number of Old Testament verses about mercy.[11] A western mindset often leans toward the questions involving how and what, while an eastern mind contemplates why and who. So if it's not in the story, that gives us a clue that our focus should be elsewhere.

There's one thing to note before we move on: the text clarifies Jesus wrote with His finger. I think that's significant. The Ten Commandments were written by the finger of God (Ex. 31:18; Deut. 9:10). So the scribes and Pharisees were challenging the writer of the law. While Jesus's words in the dirt are not revealed, we do get a glimpse into His authority as the Author of the standards the religious leaders were attempting to use to trap Him.

> **Knowing Jesus has the authority to judge, how does His response to the woman reflect how Jesus deals with your sin?**

R. C. Sproul states, "This is the only mention in Scripture of Jesus writing anything."[9]

Notice that Jesus's finger was not pointed in accusation at the woman. This confrontation started with the Law of Moses and ended with the law of Christ. Jesus shifted the hostility of the religious leaders from the woman to Himself, exchanging grace for disgrace. He offered up

His life to pay the price of sin on the cross—for the woman caught in adultery and for us. We can savor peace as we view our sin in light of His finished work of atonement.

SIN NO MORE

Jesus was the One worthy to throw a stone, but He didn't. He didn't condemn the woman, but He also didn't overlook her self-destructive lifestyle. He instructed her to turn from sin because He knew its destructive power and its deathly penalty which He would take upon Himself. His grace and truth echoes into our own battles with sin. So let's transfer the energy we use beating ourselves up to cultivating a heart of repentance.

Turning from sin and turning to God needs to be a daily practice. Take time now to bring your sins before God and ask for His help in turning in a new direction. Feel free to journal your prayer below.

PRAYER

Jesus, I may not know what you wrote in the dirt that day, but I know you have the authority to judge. Thank you for not condemning me. Help me to think about the cross and the sacrifice you made for my sin more frequently. Jesus, your kindness leads me to repentance. Today, I turn from my sin and turn to you. Reveal your grace and truth to me. In Jesus's name, Amen.

STOP AND SAVOR

Today we focused on this truth: *Jesus won't condemn you, so you can stop condemning yourself.*

What's one thing you hope to remember about what you studied today?

What words of grace and truth is God speaking to you currently?

Day Four

TRUE FREEDOM

I recently discovered that more than four hundred types of phobias exist![12] Some sound strange, like fear of cheese or fear of developing a phobia. Others, like fear of heights or public speaking, don't surprise me. I did a quick personal inventory to determine if I have any phobias and realized my tendency toward claustrophobia. If a family member puts his or her arm or leg on me while we are watching a movie, I have to get it off so I can breathe. I know it's weird, but it's one of the areas where I crave freedom.

> **If you had to pick one area where you don't like having constraints, would it be free time, free speech, freedom of physical movement, or something else?**

In our culture, freedom is often defined as the ability to do anything we want. Today, we will discover that true freedom includes the ability to say no to the short-term pleasures of sin and yes to the long-term peace found only through Christ.

I write those words understanding the tension of how hard it is to overcome sin—especially the repetitive ones. It can feel like a game of Whac-A-Mole™. We experience freedom in one area only to find ourselves enslaved in another. As we get into the text, be gentle with yourself. Rather than concentrate on areas of past failure, focus on future freedom.

THE LIGHT OF THE WORLD

READ JOHN 8:12-20 and finish the sentence below in your own words:

Because Jesus is the Light of the world, those who follow Him _____
_____.

BIG IDEA
True freedom includes the ability to say no to the short-term pleasures of sin and yes to long-term peace found only through Christ.

Life is a key word in John and points us back to the prologue (John 1:4–5).

During the Festival of Tabernacles, four massive lamps in the temple's court of women provided light where a great celebration took place every evening.[13] This illumination served as a reminder for the people of the pillar of fire that led their ancestors in the wilderness.[14] Jesus used the illustration of light—a common metaphor in the Old Testament (Ps. 89:15; Prov. 13:9; Isa. 5:20; 51:4) to reveal that while the lamps would be extinguished after the festival, His light would continue forever.[15]

This is the second of seven I AM statements recorded in John's Gospel. The first was Jesus's revelation as the Bread of Life. As the Light of the world, Jesus brings brightness but also exposure. Light reveals what sinners like to hide in the darkness.

As you evaluate your thoughts, your media choices, and your words, what does God's light of both conviction and hope expose and encourage in your life?

Which of your patterns and habits are bringing life and which are bringing death to your relationships, spiritual growth, and/or physical health?

There is double meaning in Jesus's reference to being lifted up. He would be lifted up on the cross but also lifted up to the Father, returning to the glory He enjoyed with the Father before the incarnation.[16]

Jesus came to bring us light and life—not just for a temporary event or experience—but forever. However, many in the crowd had questions about His bold claims.

DEPENDENT ON THE FATHER

READ JOHN 8:21-30 and describe in your own words the relationship between Jesus and the Father.

Jesus modeled what it meant to live in dependence on the Father. If He—fully man but also God incarnate—totally relied on the Father, how much more should we lean on Him in our neediness?

Identify at least one way you can better depend on God in the days ahead.

If you had trouble answering the previous question, don't worry. The last part of chapter 8 reveals practical truths to shape our understanding of what it means to live reliant on God.

TRUTH THAT BRINGS FREEDOM

READ JOHN 8:31-59 and answer the following questions:

What did Jesus say is the mark of a true disciple (v. 31)?

Summarize what Jesus said about freedom in verses 32-36.

What do those who belong to God gladly do (v. 47)?

Verse 30 reveals that many believed in Him, but in the following verses, Jesus showed their faith to be superficial belief. The crowd believed Jesus as long as He didn't clash with their prejudices and religious bias. The Jews grasped for freedom in their ancestry to Abraham, but real freedom is found only in Christ, because as He said, He Himself is the God of Abraham (v. 58).

This reminds us again of our memory verse this week—to look beneath the surface so we can judge correctly.

Is there something you know the Bible says to do and you aren't doing it? Is there something the Bible says not to do and you know you are doing it? Explain.

Taking the time to evaluate our thoughts is important because truth gets muddy in our chaotic world. Culture attempts to reshape our worldview and ultimately our values. We struggle to live in the truth that brings freedom. When I first read this passage, I was discouraged by the disparity I confronted: Jesus's light, my darkness; His dependence on the Father, my independence; His call to truth, my clinging to lies that lead to bondage. I identified with the crowd, full of excuses and questions. Perhaps you relate.

The good news is that our struggles don't condemn us, and we don't have to fix our failures on our own. Jesus reminds us we were created for connection with our Creator—a connection He established through His sacrifice. As we repent and obey, God continues to conform us to the image of His Son.

We won't find peace in defending our positions or arguing over nuances. Peace is found in the light. Today we can embrace afresh our neediness of Him and grow in the truth that brings freedom.

STOP AND SAVOR

Today we focused on this truth: *True freedom includes the ability to say no to the short-term pleasures of sin and yes to long-term peace found only through Christ.*

What's one thing you hope to remember about what you studied today?

How are you inspired to walk in freedom today?

Day Five
PATIENT WITH SPIRITUAL BLINDNESS

I'll never forget the drive home from getting my glasses when I was in fifth grade. I commented to my mom that I could see all the branches on the trees. Before I got glasses I viewed trees from a distance as blobs without detail. I thought everyone did. Only when I got corrective lenses did I realize what my eyes had failed to see. In our study of John 9 today, we'll discover we can have spiritual blind spots. When I say blind spots, I'm talking about things in our lives that block or hinder us from seeing the truth clearly. When we recognize these weaknesses, Jesus can open our eyes to see our need for Him.

> **READ JOHN 9:1-12.** What stands out to you about Jesus's words or actions from this account?

Jesus physically healed this man, but this healing reveals the spiritual blind spots of the disciples where they lacked awareness because of a skewed perspective. They saw the man as an opportunity for a theological discussion rather than a person in need of compassion (John 9:2). Along with most people at that time, they sourced suffering, including blindness, with personal sin.[17]

As we look at the response of the Pharisees, the man's parents, and the man himself—we'll discover that viewing a situation through the wrong lens can lead to blind spots. We can miss seeing a situation clearly when our perspective is skewed from looking through a lens of criticism, fear, insecurity, pride, selfishness, or some other negatively influencing filter.

THE LENS OF CRITICISM

> **READ JOHN 9:13-34.** Who saw this situation through the lens of criticism, and how did they express it (vv. 16,24,28-29,34)?

SCRIPTURE FOCUS
John 9

BIG IDEA
When we recognize our spiritual blindness, Jesus can open our eyes to see our need for Him.

Making the mud would have been equated with the kneading of bread, which was forbidden on the Sabbath. Later the Talmud (commentary on Jewish Law) would specify the making of mud as a violation of Sabbath rest.[18]

Seeing things through the lens of criticism caused the Pharisees to miss the peace of God through His sent One. We may not be opposing Jesus like the Pharisees, but we must still fight against a critical spirit. I personally struggle with the lens of criticism. I don't want to elevate rules over relationships or embrace a fault-finding posture, but I'm constantly fighting against these tendencies.

Is seeing things through the lens of criticism a struggle for you? If so, how?

Pastor and author Edward Klink said, "The statement that 'he is old enough' is an idiom which expresses that a person is of the legal age to speak on his own behalf."[19]

THE LENS OF FEAR

When questioned, what was the parents' response to the miracle, and why did they respond this way (vv. 22-23)?

Being banned from the synagogue was rare in Jesus's day, but it was severe.[20] The synagogue was central to Jewish life. To be banned would carry consequences for a Jewish family's livelihood, social status, and religious community. These parents avoided answering the Pharisees' questions out of fear.

How does fear impact your willingness to obey Christ or share about Him?

Maybe you struggle to share the gospel with someone, to follow a prompting of the Holy Spirit, or give because of fear. I relate to these struggles. Instead of beating yourself up about it, bring your fears to the Lord.

Ask God to reveal where you might be wearing the lens of fear rather than faith. Lay those fears before Him and ask for help to walk in faith and boldness.

THE LENS OF FAITH

Summarize the healed man's second encounter with the Pharisees. Note his proclamation, explanation, and challenge to them (vv. 24-34).

The man didn't have all the answers. He didn't know whether Jesus was a prophet or if He was a sinner. But he knew that he had been blind and now he could see. He took what he did know to be true about Jesus and proclaimed it. His testimony reminds us we don't have to have all the answers to be a witness.

READ JOHN 9:35-41. Explain what took place between Jesus and the healed man.

The healed man had received physical sight earlier, but he gained spiritual sight when he declared, "Lord, I believe!" (v. 38). Jesus patiently declared that He is the light that allows each of us to see God clearly. We can either continue to struggle with blind spots or put on the lens of faith and ask God to open our eyes to Him at work all around us.

I didn't realize how skewed my physical vision was until I got glasses. In the same way, sin distorts our view of the world, our own righteousness, and God. While all of us may not need corrective lenses for physical vision, all of us need God glasses to illuminate our path spiritually. True sight is contingent on recognizing our spiritual blindness.

STOP AND SAVOR

Today we focused on this truth: *When we recognize our spiritual blindness, Jesus can open our eyes to see our need for Him.*

What's one thing you hope to remember about what you studied today?

PRAYER

Jesus, you are the Healer. Please restore my sight spiritually so that I can see you clearly. Thank you for your patience with me as you make me aware of blind spots that need attention. Lord, I know I need your help to see. Shine your light on the path ahead of me today. In Jesus's name, Amen.

BEGIN

What's your favorite drink to order at a coffee shop?

Circle the emotion that best describes how you feel about your time with God this week. Share your answer with the group.

Happy   Content   Anxious   Sad   Angry

If you could use any color to describe how you feel about life in general right now, what would it be? Why?

Review the big ideas from this session. Which one did you enjoy the most? If any, which one did you struggle to relate to?

Based on your study from John 7–9, what are two qualities of Jesus that stand out to you?

As a group, review your memory verse from this session (John 7:24).

Choose one person to pray over the group and for your discussion time, that it would be beneficial for everyone and honoring to God.

REVIEW & DISCUSS

When it comes to meeting someone for the first time, what is your initial reaction?

●————————————————————————●————————————————————————●

Stranger danger!   *Curious, but kind*   *Can we be BFFs?*

Describe a time when you totally misjudged someone or a situation.

Why is it important to "look beneath the surface," as our memory verse reminds us?

Based on your study this week, do you think the Pharisees were good at living out that verse? Why?

READ JOHN 8:1-11. How did the Pharisees miss their own blind spots in this story while pointing out the faults of the woman?

When have you caught yourself pointing out the sins of others but neglecting to confess the sin in your heart?

How does Jesus show Himself as the Light of the world in this story?

REFLECT & APPLY

Think about your favorite drink. If it's not water, why can't you only drink that for every meal of every day?

If Jesus is the only one who can satisfy our spiritual thirst, how would it impact us to deprive ourselves from spending time with Him daily?

What does it look like in your day-to-day life to be satisfied in Jesus?

Think about the color you chose to describe how you feel. Take some time to get beyond the surface of why you feel that way. Share with the group or journal in the space below.

Write down the names of two godly people in your life you can ask this week to share any potential spiritual blind spots you have.

Grab a note card, then write down this session's memory verse: John 10:10. Discuss one or two ways that will help you memorize this verse before the next group time.

CLOSE

Get into pairs of two, then spend time sharing prayer requests and praying for each other. If you need to confess places in your life where you've been walking in darkness, ask your partner to pray specifically for those things.

Before Next Time

HERE'S WHAT YOU'LL BE WORKING ON:
- Watch Session 5 Video
- Complete Session 5 Personal Study Days (as best you can!)
- Memorize John 10:10

5

Peace in the Purposes of Jesus

The thief's purpose is to steal and kill and destroy. My purpose is to give them a rich and satisfying life.

John 10:10

Day One

AN ABUNDANT AND SATISFYING LIFE

SCRIPTURE FOCUS

John 10

BIG IDEA

Jesus is the door to an abundant and satisfying life.

Today in John 10, we will focus on how Jesus is the door to us experiencing an abundant and satisfying life.

ENTERING IN

READ JOHN 10:1-10 and write what you learn about each of these:

The shepherd
The sheep
Thieves and robbers
Jesus's purpose

Thieves and robbers were classified differently in ancient law. Thieves were criminals who broke in, while robbers were those who lived in the wild and assaulted people passing by!

Let's review a few facts about shepherding during the time of Jesus that might help us gain greater understanding as we approach the text:

- Sheep were often herded into a walled enclosure at night to protect them from predators.[2]

- The shepherd's body literally served as the door of the enclosure. He slept across the opening to keep sheep in and predators out.

- Sometimes shepherds combined their flocks into a large fold and had one doorkeeper serve as the gate of protection.[3]

- Near-Eastern shepherds called their own sheep and assembled their flocks with each sheep recognizing the master's particular call.[4]

- Sheep responded to their shepherds' voice but not to the voice of a stranger.[5]

Which of these facts is the most interesting to you?

Jesus said He is "the gate" (v. 7, CSB, NIV, NLT; or "the door," ESV, NKJV). He is the protector of the sheep and keeps the enemy at bay. He is also the only entrance into His sheepfold. And those who enter His flock will be saved and find freedom, protection, and provision. Jesus, the protecting and providing Good Shepherd, stands in contrast to the thief.

While the thief comes "to steal and kill and destroy" (v. 10), Jesus came to give us life. Perhaps your translation of John 10:10 says "life . . . to the full" (NIV), "life . . . in abundance" (CSB), or "a rich and satisfying life" (NLT). The Greek word that describes life in this verse is *perissos* and means, "exceeding some number or measure or rank or need."[6] Jesus wasn't just talking about giving us a better life experience but giving us life from God found in Him.

Would you say you're experiencing the abundant life that Jesus offers? Why or why not?

Maybe you feel like your difficulties are exceeding your satisfaction. Jesus didn't promise overflowing wealth or material possession. Nor did He promise a perfect or easy life. But He did promise life beyond what we can imagine—life filled with joy, purpose, and meaning, more internal satisfaction rather than external affluence. This fits what we've learned about savoring peace in our journey through John's Gospel; it's more an internal posture, a tranquil state of the soul, than an external state of calm circumstances.

The thief metaphor is associated with Satan, whose intent is to destroy rather than preserve life (John 8:44; 1 Pet. 5:8; 1 John 3:8).

READ JOHN 10:11-21 and record how the Good Shepherd is described versus how the hired hand is described.

GOOD SHEPHERD	HIRED HAND
Verse 11	Verse 12
Verses 14-15	Verse 13

While good shepherds serve their flocks in many ways, John emphasized that Jesus came to lay down His life for His sheep. He's not only the Shepherd who leads, He's the Shepherd who serves, sacrificially. That's why we can trust His voice.

Ezekiel 34 is a passage where God rebukes the "shepherds, the leaders of Israel" (v. 2), the religious leaders at the time who slaughtered the choice animals, clothed themselves in wool, and failed to care for the flock.[7]

It was a rare occurrence for Palestinian shepherds to die in service of sheep. When they did, it was always by accident.[8] Yet five times in this account Jesus clearly referenced His sacrificial death (John 10:11,15,17-18).

What is the role of sheep according to verses 14 and 16?

Sheep know and listen to their master. They need guidance and protection. In the same way, we need the Good Shepherd to lead us. Without Him, we are lost. Yet, too often I listen to the voices of culture, other people, or my own fickle feelings.

Mark the scale below to describe how well you are listening to the Good Shepherd's direction.

Never Listen   Sometimes Listen   Always Listening

FOLLOWING HIS VOICE

READ JOHN 10:22-42. Who knows the voice of Jesus?

What do these verses say Jesus does for His sheep?

Describe the people's reaction to Jesus explaining who He was. Why do you think they responded like that?

What's one way you can be intentional about following the voice of the Good Shepherd this week?

Whatever your action step is, remember that Jesus calls us to enter in, listen, and follow His voice. He is the door to a rich and satisfying life.

STOP AND SAVOR

Today we focused on this truth: *Jesus is the door to an abundant and satisfying life.*

What's one thing you hope to remember about what you studied today?

What characteristics of Jesus as a Shepherd stand out to you and why?

PRAYER

Lord, you are the door, the Good Shepherd, and the Son of God. Help me not to oversaturate my ears with other voices so that I can't hear yours. Lord, I am your sheep. I need direction, protection, and provision. Please guide me today. Help me to listen to and follow your voice. In Jesus's name, Amen.

Day Two

GOD'S GLORY

SCRIPTURE FOCUS

John 11

Can you recall a time when you struggled to understand God's timing in your life, specifically when you felt like you were waiting on Him to come through for you? Journal about that below.

BIG IDEA

With God, what feels like a pointless pause to us can have a powerful purpose.

Waiting often seems pointless, even painful at times. Yet God has powerful purposes in pauses.

THE DELAY

READ JOHN 11:1-16 and identify two purposes for Jesus's delay.

Verse 4

Verse 15

Jesus's first of seven signs in the Gospel of John occurred at a wedding, and His last took place at a funeral.

Jesus wasn't aimlessly wandering through His ministry just reacting to the applause of crowds or the threats of the Jewish leaders. He had purpose in all He did. His intentional delay in coming to Lazarus was to bring glory to the Father and lead His disciples to true faith in Him.

Once Jesus expressed His intention to go to Bethany, the disciples protested.

What was their concern according to verse 8?

Lazarus's sickness must have been serious for his sisters to reach out to Jesus. They lived in Bethany, only two miles from Jerusalem. The last time in Jerusalem, Jesus faced the threat of arrest and stoning (John 10:22-39). But this did not deter Him. Jesus didn't operate from fear; He followed the will of His Father.

John's Gospel gives us the best glimpse into Jesus's understanding of His timeline. He was in sync with the Father's purposes. As we consider our own lives, we can savor peace in knowing that God is never late or early.

What good purposes have come out of waiting seasons in your life?

We may encounter seasons when it feels like God didn't show up or allowed something devastating to happen. Even in these times, God can receive glory and our faith can be strengthened as we trust His purposes over what makes sense to us.

THE DECLARATION

READ JOHN 11:17-32 and summarize what Jesus told Martha in verses 25-26.

Martha was grieving and struggling to reconcile the death of her brother with the claims of Jesus. Jesus asked her if she believed His words. Not just that she believed in a coming resurrection, but that He is the resurrection. We must also consider what we believe. Does this truth guide the direction and purpose of our lives?

We can savor the peace of Jesus because He is the source of resurrection life. Even in death—our own or those we love—we can savor peace knowing that we pass from earthly life to eternal life if we belong to Jesus.

usually a large group of people—family, friends, and perhaps hired mourners— accompanied a body being taken to the grave. The mourning for the dead usually lasted several days after the burial.⁹

THE DISPLAY OF EMOTION

READ JOHN 11:33-44 and identify Jesus's emotions in this text.

Why do you think Jesus was troubled?

Let's look at the two Greek words used in verse 33 to better understand Jesus's emotions.

1. The text first says Jesus was "deeply moved in [his] spirit" (CSB, ESV, NIV), "groaned in the spirit" (NKJV), "a deep anger welled up within him" (NLT). This phrase is the Greek word *enebrimesato*, which literally means "to snort like a horse" and "generally connotes anger."[10] Most commentators agree Jesus was not angry at Mary or Martha but at death itself.

2. The text then adds that Jesus was "troubled" (CSB, NIV, NKJV), "deeply troubled" (NLT), "greatly troubled" (ESV), which is translated from the Greek word *etaraxen* which "expresses agitation, confusion, or disorganization."[11] Jesus was not apathetic in the situation. He shared in the common feeling of grief with those He loved.

Jesus knew God's glory and peoples' belief were godly purposes for His delay, but Jesus is as fully human as He is God. Mary wept, the mourners cried, and Jesus entered into their pain. Death angered Him and its painful affects grieved Him. He expressed human emotions, including tears.

What emotions have been surfacing in your life this week?

Give yourself biblical permission to express feelings, whether they are celebratory, apathetic, or overflowing with grief. Just a word of caution: while our feelings aren't sinful, sometimes the way we express them can be. Be careful that your emotional expressions don't present unwise decisions, hurtful words, or wrong behavior.

Jesus didn't lack faith; He felt and expressed human emotions.

THE DELIBERATIONS

READ JOHN 11:45-57 and record the different responses to Jesus raising Lazarus from the dead.

VERSE	PERSON/ PEOPLE	RESPONSE
Verse 45	Many people	
Verse 46	Some people	
Verses 47-48	Leading priests and Pharisees	
Verses 49-50	Caiaphas	
Verse 53	Jewish leaders	

Each of us must decide whether we believe in Jesus.

STOP AND SAVOR

Today we focused on this truth: *With God, what feels like a pointless pause to us can have a powerful purpose.*

What's one thing you hope to remember about what you studied today?

How are you challenged to wait on God's timing based on today's passage?

Day Three

DEATH

SCRIPTURE
FOCUS

John 12

My friends, Jimmy and Kelly, felt led by God to pursue an international adoption. In preparation for the adoption, Jimmy met with a good friend who had adopted a child under similar circumstances to ask about what hard things he should expect.

His friend didn't sugarcoat it. He told Jimmy he could expect to die to his own desires when it came to things like sleep, entertainment, and purchases. But he reminded him that the gospel is about dying to self.

BIG IDEA

The way to life requires death.

When we pursue gospel obedience, it often feels a little bit like dying—to our comfort, our expectations, and our agendas. As we examine the purposes of Jesus in this week's study, we'll see that for Jesus to be the resurrection and the life, He had to die.

PURPOSE OF PREPARATION

READ JOHN 12:1-11 and match the person with the description.

The man Jesus raised from the dead	Judas Iscariot
The woman serving dinner	Jesus
The woman who anointed Jesus's feet	Leading priests
The disciple who criticized the woman	Mary
The one who said to leave the woman alone	Lazarus
The group of people who wanted to kill Lazarus	Martha

What details stood out to you from this text?

In Jesus's day, it was not uncommon to spend lavishly for a funeral, including the cost of perfumes to hide the smell of decay.[12] But Mary was pouring out an expensive fragrance on Jesus while He was still alive. Jesus knew Mary's deed had great purpose—she was symbolically preparing Him for His death.

> **Sometimes circumstances in our lives can be puzzling. Can you look back and see how a particular circumstance, perhaps even a painful one, served a greater purpose in your life? If so, jot a note about it below.**

The cost of the perfume would have been an enormous sum—equivalent to a year's wages. Either Mary and her family were wealthy or the perfume could have been a family heirloom.[13]

I remember when a conflict with close friends revealed patterns of gossip and selfishness in my life. It wasn't a fun season, but it led me to repentance and a more intimate walk with the Lord. Difficult circumstances can be a catalyst that leads us to die to self in order to live to God. God's purposes in our circumstances are not to harm us. Rather, He leads us to die to self so that we may discover a rich and satisfying life in close relationship with Him.

PURPOSE OF PEACE

> **READ JOHN 12:12-19 and either sketch the scene or describe it in your own words below.**

The triumphal entry of Jesus into Jerusalem is one of the few events recorded in all four Gospels (Matt. 21:1–11; Mark 11:1–11; Luke 19:29–38).

The crowds wanted a warrior king but Jesus's entrance made it clear that was not His purpose at this time. By riding in on a donkey, Jesus presented Himself as one coming in peace, not to lead the people in a revolt against Rome. This type of entrance would serve to quell any "nationalistic expectations."[14]

Peace wasn't coming in the way the disciples, the crowd, or the religious leaders expected. They wanted political peace. Jesus was bringing peace with God.

The peace Jesus brings comes in unexpected ways in our lives as well. Sometimes, we experience peace just by recognizing our need for God in the midst of grief, conflict, or unmet expectations. Through disruption we often see beyond earthly circumstances to heavenly priorities.

In what ways has Jesus brought unexpected peace into your life?

PURPOSE IN SUFFERING

READ JOHN 12:20-36 and explain what you think the statement in the following verses means.

VERSE(S)	STATEMENT	REFLECT ON THE MEANING
Verse 24	An unplanted seed remains alone.	
Verse 25	Those who love their lives will lose it.	
Verses 27-28	Father, save me from this hour.	

The Greeks were
likely God-fearing
Gentiles who came
to worship at the
Feast of the Passover.
It's possible they
approached Philip
because he had a
Greek name.[5]

Verse 35	Those who walk in darkness can't see where they're going.	

John repeated the contrast of light and darkness throughout his Gospel (John 1:4–9; 3:19–21; 8:12; 12:35–36,46).

Jesus used several illustrations to help His listeners understand the purpose of His suffering and death. In a farming society, planting and harvesting would have been familiar to the whole community. Jesus pointed out that a seed is weak and useless until it dies. Only then does it fulfill its purpose.

Throughout John's account, Jesus has been saying that His hour had not yet come. However, when the Greeks asked for an audience with Jesus, He signaled that His hour had come. He was deeply troubled by it because He knew His purpose in coming: He came to die.

Despite the agony ahead, Jesus trusted that His death would be a doorway to life. When we choose to follow Christ, we understand gospel purposes are not accomplished by loving this life. This isn't self-hatred but turning our attention to something bigger than just the pleasures of today.

Jesus taught that the way to real life is death. Jimmy's friend from our opening story reminds us that some things are hard but worth it.

PURPOSE OF BELIEF

READ JOHN 12:37-50. What did Jesus say was His purpose (v. 46)?

Jesus told the crowd that trusting Him was trusting God. But despite seeing the miracles, many hardened their hearts in unbelief. Others did believe but feared the repercussions from the Pharisees, so they didn't commit to follow Him. They had a superficial rather than a sincere belief. Jesus doesn't force Himself on anyone, but He invites each of us to believe in Him.

How is Jesus calling you to trust Him more fully in the midst of your current circumstances?

Jesus's purpose was not accomplished without His death. Our calling is also contingent on our willingness to die—to deny ourselves and give up our lives to follow. In this we will discover real life as we live for Him.

STOP AND SAVOR

Today we focused on this truth: *The way to life requires death.*

What's one thing you hope to remember about what you studied today?

What of Jesus's words and interactions stood out to you and why?

Day Four

SERVING

What are some ways you have served others that brought you joy?

How have others served you, and how has their service been a blessing to you?

SCRIPTURE FOCUS

John 13:1–17

BIG IDEA

Jesus came to serve, and we can savor peace in following His example.

Serving can take many shapes—like mowing a neighbor's lawn, tending a sick family member, or holding babies in the church nursery. For Jesus, it included washing dirty feet.

HUMILITY

READ JOHN 13:1-5 and fill in the blanks:

- **This happened before the _____ celebration.**
- **Jesus knew that His _____ had come to leave this world.**
- **Jesus knew His _____ had given Him authority to come to earth and now return to heaven.**
- **Jesus got up from the table and began to _____ His disciples' feet.**

Chapter 13 begins what scholars refer to as Jesus's farewell discourse (John 13–17). In these first five verses we see that Jesus wasn't a victim of circumstances. He clearly understood the decisive end to His public ministry initiated the sequence of events leading up to the cross. The unbelieving crowds were gone, and Jesus reemphasized His love for His disciples. They would be the focus of His final teachings.

How do you see Jesus's humility lived out in verse 5?

This was a private gathering so it's likely no servants were on hand to wash feet. None of the disciples volunteered to perform what was considered a lowly task. In fact, Luke informs us that the disciples were arguing over who would be the greatest in the kingdom of God as they sat at the table (Luke 22:24). Jesus's wordless, humble gesture would have rebuked their attitudes. Also, His washing of feet was much more significant than merely meeting an immediate need. This act foreshadowed the cross—the selfless service Jesus exhibited to the point of death.

HOLINESS

> **READ JOHN 13:6-11** and write your personal impressions of Peter's protests and Jesus's responses below.

I love how Peter is an all-or-nothing kind of guy. He initially opposed Jesus degrading Himself but then wanted an entire scrubbing. It's clear Peter didn't quite fathom what Jesus was doing. That's understandable, since even today scholars disagree on the meaning of Jesus's words. The way I see it, Jesus used the washing of feet as an illustration of sanctifying spiritual cleansing.

Salvation isn't just a past experience; it's also a present reality. We have been saved from the penalty of sin (justification), we are being saved from the power of sin (sanctification), and we will be saved from the presence of sin (glorification). This picture of washing dirty feet is about holy living—sanctification—the daily process of growing in Christ as we walk in this world. We have an ongoing need for confession, repentance, and refreshing because of our continual struggle with sin, even after we've been saved. We don't need to be saved over and over again because our relationship with God through Christ is eternally secure. We just need cleansing restoration when we break fellowship with the Lord.

Jesus knew Peter would betray Him and get His feet dirty again and again. He would fail at critical moments. This washing of feet would provide hope on the other side of failure.

Where do you need cleansing today in your struggle with the power of sin? What keeps getting your feet dirty?

These verses give me hope that Jesus knows about my dirty feet. He understands my bent toward sin but washes me and gives me the power to change. We will never be sinless this side of heaven, but by receiving His cleansing, He restores us and reminds us of His power in us to sin less as we mature in our relationship with Him.

How does Peter's dialogue with Jesus give you hope as you consider your own sanctification process?

HELPING

READ JOHN 13:12-17 and record Jesus's instructions in verses 14-15 in your own words.

Though the disciples were focused on the levels of their greatness, Jesus showed that following Him meant not being above the lowest job. Not much has changed when it comes to people seeking greatness over humility. But Jesus set the tone of servant leadership for every one of us who claim Him as Savior. We are not here to be served but to serve.

As you reflect on Jesus's example and command regarding serving, consider where you are currently serving in your family, church, and community, and list a few examples below:

- _____

- _____

- _____

I've filled in those blanks differently over the years. Some years I would have written "changing diapers, helping with homework, and meal prep." Currently, I mentor an at-risk student at my local high school, lead a Bible study, and serve family members and friends as needed.

Consider the following questions and ask the Lord to prompt you by His Spirit with any action steps you need to take. Journal your answers below.

Is the Lord calling you to make an attitude adjustment when it comes to serving? If so, in what way?

What needs have you noticed around you (home, church, community, etc.) that you could meet?

Serving can be about as glamorous as washing dirty feet, but it can be a vehicle on the road to fulfilling our God-given purpose. Two of my children have now served as staffers at a family camp. They would tell you those seasons of serving were physically exhausting but spiritually enriching. Often, we seek peace through entertainment or consuming more stuff, but it never ultimately satisfies. Jesus says we will be fulfilled as we pour out our lives in humility, holiness, and helping others.

STOP AND SAVOR

Today we focused on this truth: *Jesus came to serve, and we can savor peace in following His example.*

What's one thing you hope to remember about what you studied today?

What stands out to you about Jesus's words and actions from today's Scripture?

What is one tangible way you can serve someone today? How will that help you savor the peace of Jesus?

Jesus, though you are God, you didn't consider yourself above the lowest task. Make me like you. Break my selfishness and pride and give me eyes to see the needs around me and energy to pour out my life in service. Change my attitude so that I might discover peace in living for you and serving others rather than seeking my own momentary pleasure. In Jesus's name, Amen.

Day Five
LOVE

SCRIPTURE FOCUS

John 13:18–35

BIG IDEA

Jesus teaches us to love and be loved.

The usual arrangement at a meal in Jesus's day was to have a series of couches forming a U-shape around a low table with the host placed at the center and the most honored guests on His immediate right and left side.[17]

Our culture is in love with love. We love pizza. We love comfy clothes. We love our friends. If we aren't careful, the word *love* can fall prey to overuse that robs the word of its significance.

How would you define *love*?

Maybe you said something like strong admiration or unconditional affection. The Greek word for "love" we will encounter in today's text is *agapao,* one of several Greek words for love. It's a verb that "refers to a pure, willful, sacrificial love that intentionally desires another's highest good."[16] That's not something we feel about food or fads, but a love we supernaturally receive from God and share with others.

As we close out our week of study focused on savoring peace in the purposes of Jesus, we will find no greater purpose than love. Jesus loved His disciples and commands us to love as He loved.

LOVING ALL THE WAY

READ JOHN 13:18-30 and answer the following questions:

Why did Jesus tell the disciples about His betrayer ahead of time (v. 19)?

What emotion did Jesus experience as He anticipated His betrayal (v. 21)?

After Judas ate, what pace did Jesus encourage him to take (v. 27)?

We saw in the previous day of study that Jesus washed the disciples' dirty feet, including those of Judas. Many scholars suggest that Judas may have been seated in the place of honor on Jesus's left since Jesus was able to speak to him privately.[18] So, Jesus honored Judas, possibly with a special seat and certainly by offering him the morsel of bread.[19] While Judas received the food, he did not receive the love. Instead, he quickly proceeded into literal and spiritual darkness.

Jesus loved even those who opposed Him. We should follow His example in loving all the way.

> **What is a practical way you can show love to someone with whom you have a complicated relationship?**

AN IDENTITY OF LOVE

> **RE-READ JOHN 13:23.** How is the person sitting next to Jesus at the table described? Who do you think this is?

This is the first mention of the "beloved disciple," who most scholars agree is John, the author of this Gospel. This description will be repeated at the cross (19:26-27), the empty tomb (20:2), the Sea of Tiberias when Jesus appeared in resurrected body (21:20), and implied in the final two verses of the book (21:24-25).

Why John described himself in that way is unknown. But we do know John understood and received the love that motivated God to send Jesus (John 3:16). John wasn't displaying arrogance. Instead, he was likely expressing his indebtedness to grace. One commentator said the description was John's "quiet way of refusing to give even the impression of sharing a platform with Jesus."[20]

Jesus transformed John's life, and John wanted to give Him all the glory. In the same way, God has changed our lives, and we can now see ourselves as loved by God, even though we don't always feel loved.

My dad died from Stage 4 cancer during the writing of this study. I remember when we first got the news, I often found myself troubled and crying from grief. But like Jesus, who knew He was loved by the Father even as He moved toward the cross of suffering, we can identify ourselves as loved by God as we endure difficulties like cancer, sorrow, and death.

> **Take a moment to remember who and whose you are. Write your name in the blanks below. Then meditate on these truths:**
>
> **_____ is loved by God. Jesus suffered and died to give His life for _____ in order to restore her relationship with the Father.**

If you have committed your life to Jesus, you are His beloved disciple. John understood his position, and we can too. We are loved.

LOVING AS JESUS LOVED

Jesus showed us how to love. He loved Judas, and He also loved His disciples by preparing them as best He could for what was to come. The disciples would have been disoriented by Jesus's predictions about His coming suffering and betrayal, especially in light of His miracles which brought popularity and crowds. They couldn't fully appreciate what Jesus knew was coming.

> **READ JOHN 13:31-38.** Explain Jesus's new commandment in your own words.

The command to "love each other" in John 13:34 was not new (Lev. 19:18). But while the law instructed people to love each other as they love themselves, Jesus's new command is for us to love others the way He loved us. This wasn't possible until God dwelt among us and sent His Spirit to dwell in us.

Jesus said this kind of love for one another would prove to the world that we are His disciples. John wrote more about this in 1 John 4:

> If someone says, "I love God," but hates a fellow believer,
> that person is a liar; for if we don't love people we can
> see, how can we love God, whom we cannot see?
> And he has given us this command: Those who
> love God must also love their fellow believers.
> 1 JOHN 4:20-21

In what way is the Holy Spirit prompting you concerning how you love your brothers and sisters in Christ? Are you truly loving them as Jesus loves you? Are there new relationships you need to deepen? Broken ones you need to mend? Write below what comes to mind as you listen to the Lord.

We can't love others like Jesus without Jesus. Let's savor His love now and commit to sharing it abundantly.

STOP AND SAVOR

Today we focused on this truth: *Jesus teaches us to love and be loved.*

What's one thing you hope to remember about what you studied today?

How does Jesus need to help you love others like Him?

PRAYER

Jesus, I am your beloved disciple. Please help me to see myself as you see me. Sometimes loving others can be challenging. You know my struggles. Fill me so full with your love that it overflows to everyone, even the people I find hard to love. In Jesus's name, Amen.

BEGIN

What is your favorite emoji and why?

Circle the emotion that best describes how you feel about your time with God this week. Share your answer with the group.

Happy   Content   Anxious   Sad   Angry

If you could use any color to describe how you feel about life in general right now, what would it be? Why?

Review the big ideas from this session. Which one did you enjoy the most? If any, which one did you struggle to relate to?

Based on your study from John 10–13, what are two qualities of Jesus that stand out to you?

As a group, review your memory verse from this session (John 10:10).

Choose one person to pray over the group and for your discussion time, that it would be beneficial for everyone and honoring to God.

REVIEW & DISCUSS

How would you explain the purpose of life to someone?

When life gets hard and messy, does it comfort you knowing that God has a purpose for all of it? Explain.

READ JOHN 10:1-10. What stands out to you about Jesus being the Good Shepherd?

What is the responsibility of the sheep according to verse 4?

READ PSALM 23 BELOW. Underline all the things the Lord as our shepherd does for us.

The Lord is my shepherd; I have all that I need.
He lets me rest in green meadows;
he leads me beside peaceful streams.
He renews my strength.
He guides me along right paths, bringing honor to his name.
Even when I walk through the darkest valley,
I will not be afraid, for you are close beside me.
Your rod and your staff protect and comfort me.
You prepare a feast for me in the presence of my enemies.
You honor me by anointing my head with oil.
My cup overflows with blessings.
Surely your goodness and unfailing love will pursue me
all the days of my life,
and I will live in the house of the Lord forever.

REFLECT & APPLY

If we are sheep, what is our job as followers of God? What's His job?

Do you ever feel the tendency to try to do the shepherd's job rather than just obeying His voice?

How does trusting the heart of the Good Shepherd allow us to find peace in difficult situations?

What situation in your life are you struggling to trust God with? Why do you think that is?

In the space below, write down a prayer that surrenders the situation to Jesus in order to place your trust fully in Him and His good purpose for the pain. Ask Him to provide you peace and comfort in this moment.

Grab a note card, then write down this session's memory verse: John 14:27. Discuss one or two ways that will help you memorize this verse before the next group time.

CLOSE

End this time with a "popcorn prayer." Go around the circle to say a word or phrase of praise to God. If you aren't sure what to say, simply say, "Thank You, God." Then go around the circle a second time saying a word or brief phrase to express specific requests to the Lord. If you don't want to share, simply say, "I need You, God." The leader of your group can close out in prayer.

Before Next Time

HERE'S WHAT YOU'LL BE WORKING ON:
- Watch Session 6 Video
- Complete Session 6 Personal Study Days (as best you can!)
- Memorize John 14:27

6

Peace in the Promises of Jesus

I am leaving you with a gift—
peace of mind and heart.
And the peace I give is a gift
the world cannot give.
So don't be troubled
or afraid.

John 14:27

Day One
PROMISES IN TROUBLED TIMES

BIG IDEA

You can savor peace as you consider where you'll go, who you know, and what Jesus bestows.

As I mentioned earlier in the study, my father battled late-stage cancer before passing away. I remember it being such a rough season. I know hopeful truths about Jesus and resurrection life after death, yet in the same breath, my heavy heart leads to tears when I reflect on that time. I miss my dad, and I mourn for my mom, who is alone after fifty-three years of marriage.

I find comfort and see God's kindness to me personally as together we focus this week on savoring peace in the promises of Jesus in John 14–17. In these chapters, Jesus shares promises we can stand on whether we are encountering a season of intense difficulty, incredible celebration, or anything in between. We will also discover that persecution and pruning can benefit our souls.

READ JOHN 14:1 and write Jesus's instruction below.

One commentator said a good translation of Jesus's command in John 14:1 would be, "Set your heart at ease."[1]

Jesus calls us to trust Him and the Father. But how we can accomplish that, particularly when we experience difficult circumstances?

Has something been troubling your heart lately? If so, write a few words about it.

Jesus knew what trouble felt like, even before the cross. When His friend Lazarus died and Judas betrayed Him, we read that Jesus was troubled. He understands human emotion because He "became human and made his home among us" (John 1:14).

Jesus also knew His disciples were troubled. He had just revealed that one of them would betray Him (13:21) and that He was leaving them (v. 33). Certainly, Peter would have been disturbed by the news that he would deny Jesus three times before the night was over (v. 38). Yet, He told them not to let their hearts be troubled.

Jesus was saying you don't have to let your feelings boss you around. You can lament, but anxiety doesn't get the final word. Instead, you can savor peace as you consider where you'll go, Who you know, and what prayer bestows.

WHERE YOU'LL GO

READ JOHN 14:2-3. Where did Jesus says His followers will go?

Scripture uses many descriptions to speak of the next life, including "the eternal Kingdom" (2 Pet. 1:11), "an inheritance" (1 Pet. 1:4), and "a city" (Heb. 11:16). But I love how Jesus described it as "home" (John 14:2).

What are some sights, sounds, or smells that make you think of home?

"The focus of this text is not merely the place but the person; as Jesus said, each Christian will dwell in 'my Father's house.'"[2]

My slippers, cozy blanket, and a cup of tea in my favorite mug all come to my mind.

Jesus said He was preparing a place for us to be with Him forever. Keeping this in perspective gives us hope in the midst of suffering. Measuring our current problems against the hope of heaven allows us to reframe our circumstances with a new mindset.

How does thinking about where you'll go in the next life brighten your outlook today?

I'm still shedding tears knowing my dad has left this earth, but thinking about him forever dwelling in the Father's house brings me peace to savor in the midst of grief.

READ JOHN 14:4-11 and circle your answer to the following questions.

Which disciple admitted He had no idea where Jesus was going (v. 5)?

A. Phillip

B. Peter

C. Thomas

How did Jesus respond to his question (v. 6)?

A. I am the Bread of Life.

B. I am the Way, the Truth, and the Life.

C. I am the Light of the World.

How did Jesus explain His connection with the Father (vv. 7-11)?

A. If you really know me, you know the Father.

B. If you have seen me, you have seen the Father.

C. I am in the Father, and the Father is in me.

D. The words I speak are not my own but from the Father who is in me.

E. All of the above.

I love that Thomas voiced what other the disciples might have been thinking. Jesus had withdrawn at times to escape arrest. It's possible Thomas thought Jesus was referring to one of those secret places.[3] Bottom line, Thomas didn't know where Jesus was going or how to get there. Jesus responded with another I AM statement, making it clear that the way is a Person. He is the Way.

We don't have to let our hearts be troubled because of Who we know. Jesus made it clear that He and the Father are inseparable. When we know, see, and hear Jesus, we are knowing, seeing, and hearing the Father. He is our Way, our Truth, and our Life.

WHAT JESUS BESTOWS

READ JOHN 14:12-14 and fill in the blanks below. (Answers may vary according to your translation.)

Anyone who believes in Jesus will do _____
_____ (v. 12).

Ask for anything in Jesus's name, and He _____
(vv. 13-14).

Jesus invited His followers to ask for anything. He wasn't teaching that we can name and claim our desires, then He delivers like a magic genie. The text qualifies our asking—in Jesus's name. This doesn't mean we can just tack those words onto any prayer and get what we want. Jesus's name represents His character. Asking in His name means asking in line with His will.

What's striking here is the access. Jesus invites us and has made a way for us to converse with the God of creation. Through prayer, Jesus bestows on us an avenue to intimacy with God.

> **How has talking to Jesus brought you peace when you felt troubled?**

My season of grief has been full of tears, but it's also given me a nearness to the Lord that only desperation can bring. Jesus's invitation to ask Him for anything has been a precious gift to me as I've cried out for comfort, grace, and His presence. As we pray, Jesus bestows the power not to let trouble overwhelm us. The next time anxiety knocks at the door of our hearts, we can let prayer answer it![4]

STOP AND SAVOR

Today we focused on this truth: *You can savor peace as you consider where you'll go, who You know, and what Jesus bestows.*

> **What's one thing you hope to remember about what you studied today?**

> **How does Jesus's statement "I am the way, the truth, and the life" in John 14:6 encourage you?**

Lord, you are the Way, the Truth, and the Life. It blows my mind that you invite me to ask for anything. Help me to know what to ask for. Align me to your will so that I bring you glory. Help me see my troubles through the lens of where I'll go, who I know, and all that you bestow! In Jesus's name, Amen.

Day Two

THE PROMISE OF THE HOLY SPIRIT

SCRIPTURE FOCUS

John 14:15–31

BIG IDEA

Jesus never guaranteed peaceful circumstances but promised to send an Advocate to help us receive His gift of peace.

John 14–17 includes the longest teaching anywhere in Scripture concerning the ministry of the Holy Spirit, including why God sent Him and what He does in our midst.[5]

One evening around the dinner table, our family shared high and low points of the day. One of our twins, who was in third grade at the time, broke into tears as she shared her "low." A teacher had made a comment about her in front of other students that hurt her feelings. My husband asked if she wanted him to speak to the teacher about it. She nodded yes through her tears.

My husband knew that her teacher, a young man new to his profession, likely had little experience with the sensitivities of eight-year-old girls. He kindly took the teacher aside the next morning and mentioned our daughter's hurt feelings. The teacher acknowledged that he was only teasing but could see the impact of his words in the moment and wasn't sure how to handle it. He apologized to our daughter later that day.

Can you think of a time when you longed for someone to come to your defense? If so, explain.

We all need support, particularly when we feel sad, alone, or confused. The disciples certainly found themselves troubled as Jesus continued His farewell discourse around the table at the Last Supper. He spoke of difficult days ahead but also promised them an Advocate to help.

DEFENDER

READ JOHN 14:15-17 and write at least three things you discover about the Holy Spirit.

1.

2.

3.

In this passage, we encounter a Greek word for "the Holy Spirit" unique to John's Gospel—*parakletos*. It's translated "Advocate," "Counselor," or "Comforter" but literally means "a person summoned to one's aid."[6]

Notice that Jesus said He would give us another Advocate. (The Greek word translated "another" means "another of the same kind."[7]) That caused me to wonder about the identity of the other One.

> **READ 1 JOHN 2:1** below and circle the identity of the first Advocate.

> My dear children, I am writing this to you so that you
> will not sin. But if anyone does sin, we have an
> advocate who pleads our case before the Father.
> He is Jesus Christ, the one who is truly righteous.

Jesus is our Advocate, speaking to the Father in our defense. The Holy Spirit—who is not a force, but a person—would be an advocate, or helper, like Jesus.

> **How is the Holy Spirit an advocate, helper, and comforter for you?**

REMINDERS

> **READ JOHN 14:18-26** and draw a line from the beginning of the statement on the left to the correct ending on the right.

I will not abandon you as orphans	love me.
Those who obey (keep) my commandments	do what I say.
Anyone (all) who loves me will	teach and remind you of what I said.
The Holy Spirit will	I will come to you.

"The uncompromising connection between love for Christ and obedience to Christ repeatedly recurs in John's writings (cf. vv. 21,23; 15:14)."[8]

What did Jesus seem to be emphasizing to His disciples?

Jesus repeatedly connected love and obedience. These strong words can make us uncomfortable. After all, none of us obey all the commandments all the time. Yes, we love Jesus, and yet we struggle with sin. But it's not just about following the rules. Take the Pharisees. Their focus was on following all the laws, but Jesus was in constant conflict with them.

Jesus's teaching in John 14 reveals that if our obedience is lacking, we shouldn't try harder to obey. Instead, we should begin with love and faith. This is the path to peace.

Ask the Holy Spirit to reveal where your love for the Lord might need to be rekindled. What spiritual disciplines or practices would add fuel to the fire? What kinds of attitudes, thinking patterns, or actions are quenching the flames? You don't have to write anything down, just take a minute to ask the Advocate to guide you into greater awareness and deeper love.

"The pax Romana ("Roman peace") was won and maintained by a brutal sword; not a few Jews thought the messianic peace would have to be secured by a still mightier sword. Instead, it was secured by an innocent man who suffered and died at the hands of the Romans, of the Jews, and of all of us."[11]

RECEIVERS

READ JOHN 14:27-31 and describe the gift Jesus said He was leaving us.

We've already mentioned the Greek word for "peace" is *eirene*, which means "the tranquil state of a soul assured of its salvation through Christ, and so fearing nothing from God and content with its earthly lot."[9] Though the New Testament is written in Greek, these Jewish disciples would have been familiar with the Hebrew word for "peace"—*shalom*. This peace means "completeness, soundness, welfare, peace."[10]

Have you struggled to find peace lately? If so, in what way?

Although Jesus gives us His peace, we don't always walk in it. Too often we're distracted by the world and focused on the storms. What are some practical things you can do to stay centered on Christ and savor His peace?

Chaos is constant in this world until Jesus returns, but it doesn't have to be constant inside us. Instead, we can listen to our Advocate who reminds us of what Jesus promised and receive His peace!

STOP AND SAVOR

Today we focused on this truth: *Jesus never guaranteed peaceful circumstances but promised to send an Advocate to help us receive His gift of peace.*

What's one thing you hope to remember about what you studied today?

From Jesus's teaching on the Holy Spirit, what stands out most to you?

PRAYER

Jesus, thank you for sending the Advocate, the Holy Spirit, to live inside me. Help me believe all that you said and grow deeper in my understanding of your Spirit. Guide me, remind me of truth, and show me how to receive the gift of peace. I don't want to keep looking for peace from worldly things when you clearly said I won't find it there! In Jesus's name, Amen.

Day Three
A PROMISE TO PRODUCE

BIG IDEA

We need to hang in there with Jesus, so He can produce spiritual fruit in our lives.

This morning I woke up before the alarm on my phone went off. I reached over to see the time and noticed a low battery message. That seemed odd because it appeared to be plugged in. I removed the cord from the phone port and reattached it. It worked! Seems a loose connection had been the culprit. Without that proper connection, it can't provide communication, notifications, and information.

> **What other devices you use regularly need to be plugged into a power source to perform?**

PROMISE TO PRUNE

READ JOHN 15:1-8 and note who each phrase describes by using the following letters. (Some answers have more than one letter.)

J - Jesus   F- Father   D - Disciples of Jesus

_____ The true vine (v. 1)

_____ The gardener (vinedresser, husbandman) (v. 1)

_____ Cuts off unproductive branches and prunes productive branches (v. 2)

_____ Pruned and cleansed by Jesus's message (v. 3)

_____ Remains or abides (v. 4)

_____ The branches (v. 5)

_____ Apart from Christ, they can do nothing (v. 5)

_____ If they remain in Christ, and His words remain in them, they can ask for anything and receive it (v. 7)

_____ Produce much fruit and bring glory to Him (v. 8)

In the Old Testament, Israel was referred to as the vine (Ps. 80:8-18; Isa. 5:1-7; Jer. 2:21; Ezek. 15:1-5). But for the most part, Israel is being chastised for not producing fruit in these passages. Then Jesus used the vine as an illustration in His teaching (Matt. 20:1-7; Mark 12:1-11). But here in John 15:1, Jesus declared that He is "the true grapevine," and we are the branches.

> **What spiritual truths about your relationship with God emerge from this gardening illustration?**

Jesus revealed His last I AM statement recorded in the book of John: "I am the true grapevine" (John 15:1).

THE PROMISE OF FRUIT

The Greek word for "abide" or "remain" is *meno*, which means "to continue to be present."[12] *Meno* is used eleven times in the first eleven verses of John 15. We all have a tendency toward self-reliance. Using the vine illustration, Jesus tells us to hang with Him—to stay connected to Him. When we are tempted to stop praying, studying His Word, or any of the other spiritual rhythms that connect us to God, He tells us to continue to show up. When we do, He will supply the power we need to produce fruit.

> **What does abiding in Christ look like on a practical basis in your relationship with Him?**

> **How would you define *spiritual fruit*?**

Paul told the Galatians that the fruit produced in our lives when we yield to the Holy Spirit is godly character—love, peace, patience, and so forth (Gal. 5:22-23). Also in the New Testament, fruit is seen as "praise to God" (Heb. 13:15), meeting needs (Rom. 15:28), and leading people to Christ (Rom. 1:13; Col. 1:6).[13] So basically, our connection to the Vine will be evident by the fruit of character and influence. If we lack evidence of this fruit, we shouldn't beat ourselves up, strive harder, or give up. Instead, we can ask the Lord for help in reconnecting and remaining with Him.

PROMISE OF JOY

READ JOHN 15:9-17. Summarize what Jesus said about joy in verse 11.

When we abide with Him, Jesus said our joy will overflow. He wasn't talking about a feeling of happiness based on circumstances. He was talking about a sense of joy that is present even in the midst of grief, disappointment, and difficulties. Like peace, joy runs deeper than circumstances because it rests on God's character.

PROMISE OF PERSECUTION

READ JOHN 15:18-27.

Jesus doesn't want us to be caught off guard. The world rejected Him, so they will reject His followers. Knowing this ahead of time means less confusion and disillusionment. Chaos may seem to rule, but Jesus is the Logos, the Living Word, who brings order out of the chaos. The illustration of the vine shows us that, despite what we face as Christians, we can live God-honoring, fruitful lives if we remain in Him.

STOP AND SAVOR

Today we focused on this truth: *We need to hang in there with Jesus, so He can produce spiritual fruit in our lives.*

What's one thing you hope to remember about what you studied today?

Day Four
PROMISE OF PEACE

My best friend is a math teacher. Just today she was explaining to me how teaching difficult topics has to be done slowly. For example, the Pythagorean theorem requires starting with basics, repeating prior concepts of algebra, and breaking down information into smaller bites.

As I was researching today's study on John 16, I couldn't help but think of my friend's approach of going slow, explaining a little at a time, anticipating questions, and repeating herself. Jesus was in the middle of a marathon teaching loaded with difficult concepts. He had little time left and wanted to help His disciples understand the coming suffering while encouraging them to hold onto the big picture of the Father's love. He promised peace in the midst of chaos through His Spirit and prayer.

> **READ JOHN 16:1-4 and write the difficulties Jesus described.**

Can you imagine learning you will be kicked out of your church and killed by someone who thinks they're serving God by doing so? In discussing these difficult, turbulent situations, Jesus employed the method of my math teacher friend to teach, remind, and encourage His followers.

THE SPIRIT OF TRUTH

> **READ JOHN 16:5-15 and find four specific ways the Holy Spirit advocates for us:**

1. He will _____ (v. 8).

2. He will _____ (v. 13a)

3. He will tell you about the _____ (v. 13b)

4. He will bring Jesus glory by _____
   _____ (v. 14).

John 16

BIG IDEA

Jesus promised peace in the midst of chaos through His Spirit and prayer.

Let's consider how these promises from Jesus regarding the Holy Spirit intersect with our lives today.

1. CONVICT THE WORLD OF SIN, RIGHTEOUSNESS, AND JUDGMENT. The verb *convict* (*elencho*) is a legal term that means to pronounce a judicial verdict. A court can convict a man of murder, but only the Spirit can convict a person of unbelief, as only He can judge motives. If you know Christ, you have experienced the Holy Spirit's conviction, enabling you to recognize your sin and turn from it.

> **When did you first sense the Holy Spirit convicting you of sin? What was that experience like and how did you respond?**

> **Are you experiencing the Spirit's conviction today? If so, in what way and what do you need to do?**

2. GUIDE YOU INTO ALL TRUTH. The Holy Spirit, who is called "the Spirit of truth" (v. 13), will help us know and understand the truth of God as revealed in creation, the Scriptures, and especially in Christ. As we interact with Scripture, He can direct our study, bring a parallel passage to mind, or lead us to talk to a mentor or teacher. He also helps us recall memorized Scripture when we face decisions, crises, temptation, and ministry opportunities. Someone once told me memorizing Scripture is like increasing the Holy Spirit's vocabulary in your life.

> **How has the Holy Spirit recently guided you in your pursuit of truth? Be specific.**

3. TELL YOU ABOUT THE FUTURE. I often need guidance or assurance as I think about the days, months, and years ahead. The Holy Spirit doesn't speak on His own, but He tells us what He has heard. This doesn't guarantee that the Spirit will provide us with details about future personal events. It does mean He will show what is ahead for those who follow Christ, which He has done through Scripture. And as we submit to Him, He will faithfully guide us into that future.

> **What are some things the Holy Spirit has revealed about the future in Scripture that excites you? That frightens you? That challenges you?**

4. TELLING US WHAT HE RECEIVES FROM JESUS. The Holy Spirit will share with us the words of Jesus. This last promise also speaks to the source and authority by which He shares with us. He's not making things up on His own. Everything comes from Jesus, who has received all things from the Father.

> **As you consider this work of the Holy Spirit, how are you inspired to interact with Him differently?**

> **If you struggled to answer that question, here is an idea that has proved beneficial in my life. Write these four prayers on a sticky note and put it on your bathroom mirror, the dashboard of your car, or somewhere you will see it throughout the day. Then use these prayer prompts each time you see the note for the next three days:**

>   - **Holy Spirit, convict me of sin today.**
>   - **Holy Spirit, guide me into truth today.**
>   - **Holy Spirit, show me what the future holds.**
>   - **Holy Spirit, remind me of Jesus's words.**

READ JOHN 16:16-22. What were the disciples confused about (vv. 16-19)?

A. Jesus saying they wouldn't see Him and then they would in a little while.

B. Jesus saying the Holy Spirit would tell them the future.

C. Jesus saying sadness would be turned to joy.

Jesus used what example to illustrate grief being turned to joy (v. 21)?

A. A butterfly coming from a caterpillar

B. The birth of a baby

C. The growth of a plant

In these verses, Jesus was trying to prepare His friends for what was about to happen to Him. There would be pain and grief, followed by joy when they saw Him again. As we follow Christ, despite being on this side of the resurrection, we still face days of pain, sorrow, and grief. While His presence and provision carries us through these days, we long for the day when we will see Him again and all will be made right, when our sadness will forever be turned to joy.

How does the promise of His joy-filled return give new perspective to your current challenges?

Jesus lived these truths as He approached the cross, grieving the coming pain but celebrating ultimate salvation.

PRAYER

READ JOHN 16:23-33 and answer the following questions:

Who can you ask directly for your needs (v. 23)?

How does Jesus describe the Father's feelings for believers (v. 27)?

Why can we take heart and have peace in the midst of trials and sorrows (v. 33)?

Jesus emphasized that asking in His name gives us direct access to the Father, a Father who loves us. And that no matter what we go through, we can savor His peace because He has overcome the world.

STOP AND SAVOR

Today we focused on this truth: *Jesus promised peace in the midst of chaos through His Spirit and prayer.*

What's one thing you hope to remember about what you studied today?

What do you need to ask for in Jesus's name as you think about your current challenges?

Day Five

PRAYER PROMISES

SCRIPTURE
FOCUS

John 17

BIG IDEA

We can know what Jesus wants for us through His prayer for us.

In John 17, Jesus finished His farewell discourse with a prayer for Himself, His disciples, and all those who believe in Him, including you and me. In this prayer we will discover something vitally important Jesus wants for all of us.

PRAYING FOR HIMSELF

READ JOHN 17:1-5.

The first and last statements were Jesus's prayers for Himself. The other statements reveal theological truths about the work of Father and Son and provide the definition of *eternal life*—intimate knowledge of God through Christ. By beginning with praying for Himself, Jesus reminds us we can ask for God's goodness to be displayed in our lives, not for our own benefit, but for His glory.

What are you currently praying for yourself, and how is it connected to God's goodness being displayed in your life?

John 17 contains the Lord's longest recorded prayer in Scripture and is sometimes referred to as the "high priestly prayer" because of its tone of consecration.[14]

I'm asking God to help me complete the work He has given me today. This includes household tasks, answering emails, studying, writing, and resting. I'm praying that in all these things I would be faithful and bring glory to the Lord. Jesus prayed for Himself, and we can too.

PRAYING FOR HIS DISCIPLES (vv. 6-19)

The bulk of Jesus's prayer centered on His disciples.

READ JOHN 17:6-19 and list the specific requests Jesus prayed for His disciples in the following verses:

VERSE(S)	JESUS'S SPECIFIC PRAYER REQUESTS
Verse 11	
Verse 15	
Verse 17	

Jesus prayed for the disciples' protection, unity, safety, and holiness. What stands out to you from these petitions?

While we learn about prayer from this section of John 17, we also gain greater insight into the character and work of the Father and Son. Based on the verses we just read, label the following truths as describing the Father (F) or Jesus (J).

_____ He gave those who belonged to Him to Jesus (vv. 6,10).

_____ He gave Jesus His name (v. 11).

_____ He told His followers many things so they would be filled with joy (v. 13).

_____ He gave the disciples the Father's word (v. 14).

_____ He gave Himself as a sacrifice so that His followers could be made holy (v. 19).

PRAYING FOR US

In the final section of His prayer, Jesus prayed for all believers—that includes you and me!

READ JOHN 17:20-26 and list Jesus's specific prayer requests:

VERSE	JESUS'S PRAYER REQUESTS
Verse 21	
Verse 22	
Verse 23	
Verse 24	

What main theme stood out to you from Jesus's prayer for us?

Why was our unity so important to Jesus (vv. 21,23)?

Jesus prayed for unity not uniformity. He wasn't praying we would dress the same, act the same, or even agree on every nuance of our faith in cookie cutter fashion. He was praying we would be one in heart and purpose for the gospel, because evidently our unity and love for each other are key components to the effectiveness of our witness (John 13:34-35).

I can't help but feel the tension of Jesus's prayer for unity in a time when Christians seem so divided. We may disagree about baptism, women in ministry, worship styles, and a hundred other things, but we should be able to get on the same page at the foot of the cross and the empty tomb. Let the gospel be our rallying cry! When it comes to non-gospel issues, let's discuss with curiosity, study with diligence, and if needed, disagree with love. And like Jesus, pray for unity!

Let's note one other factor about unity. Go back to John 17:23, and write how much the Father loves those who believe in Jesus.

I'm just reveling in this fact right now. The Father loves us as much as He loves Jesus! The same love the Father loves Jesus with is now on us and in us. Thus, we get to participate in the loving communion with the Father, Son, and Holy Spirit. That is incredible! Seeing other believers (especially those we disagree with) framed in this understanding of how the Father loves all of us should propel us to take steps toward unity.

Who is the Lord calling you to see as a person loved by the Father today? How can you extend that love to him or her this week?

STOP AND SAVOR

Today we focused on this truth: *We can know what Jesus wants for us through His prayer for us.*

What's one thing you hope to remember about what you studied today?

How does knowing that the Father loves each of us as much as He loves Jesus shape your view of yourself? Of others?

BEGIN

Describe the taste of your favorite fruit to the group without saying what it looks like or what it's called. See how many people can guess it correctly.

Circle the emotion that best describes how you feel about your time with God this week. Share your answer with the group.

Happy   Content   Anxious   Sad   Angry

If you could use any color to describe how you feel about life in general right now, what would it be? Why?

Review the big ideas from this session. Which one did you enjoy the most? If any, which one did you struggle to relate to?

Based on your study from John 14–17, what are two qualities of Jesus that stand out to you?

As a group, review your memory verse from this session
(John 14:27).

Choose one person to pray over the group and for your discussion time, that it would be beneficial for everyone and honoring to God.

REVIEW & DISCUSS

On the scale below, how good of a promise keeper are you?

●————————————————●————————————————●

The worst ever!　　　　　　　*It depends.*　　　　　*Never broken a promise!*

When someone tells you she promises, do you believe her? Why or why not?

READ JOHN 14:15-17. Who did Jesus promise to send His disciples? For how long?

Read the verses below and match each one with a description of the Holy Spirit:

John 14:16; 15:26	*Giver of Power*
John 14:26	*Seal of Salvation*
Acts 1:8	*Counselor / Advocate*
Romans 8:26	*Peace Giver*
John 14:27	*Intercessor*
Matthew 28:19–20	*Person of the Trinity*
Ephesians 1:13	*Teacher*

REFLECT & APPLY

What did you know about the Holy Spirit before this session? How has that changed based on what you've now learned?

READ JOHN 14:26-27. How do you think the gift of peace is connected to the gift of the Holy Spirit?

What current situation in your life lacks peace?

How have you asked the Holy Spirit to give you peace in light of what you're facing?

Jesus's promise of the Holy Spirit was to prepare the disciples for what's to come, to help them stay rooted in Him, and to continue producing fruit. In what area do you need the Holy Spirit's help most today?

After discussing your answers with the group, consider getting into smaller groups to pray for one another. Discuss a few ways you can help each other remember the gift and power of the Holy Spirit at work in your lives.

Grab a note card, then write down this session's memory verse: John 20:31. Discuss one or two ways that will help you memorize this verse before the next group time.

✕ CLOSE

Choose one person to close in prayer. Spend time thanking God for keeping His promises and being with you always through the gift of the Holy Spirit.

Before Next Time

HERE'S WHAT YOU'LL BE WORKING ON:
- Watch Session 7 Video
- Complete Session 7 Personal Study Days (as best you can!)
- Memorize John 20:31

7

Peace in the Passion of Jesus

But these are written so that you may continue to believe that Jesus is the Messiah, the Son of God, and that by believing in him you will have life by the power of his name.

John 20:31

Day One

PASSION FOR A GREATER KINGDOM

SCRIPTURE
FOCUS

John 18

BIG IDEA

We can spend less time stressing over earthly pursuits when we remember that Jesus's kingdom is not of this world.

Today I mailed three bills, called two businesses, drove to a restaurant to retrieve the credit card I left there last night, sorted and filed a stack of mail, stopped by a previous address to pick up a package, and answered three thousand texts. OK, maybe it only felt like three thousand. The stuff of life can feel all-consuming at times.

What tasks or situations are currently consuming you?

These tasks are often necessary—dishwashers need unloading, papers need writing, and texts need answering! But here's the danger, if we aren't careful, these earthly concerns can crowd out our passion for God's kingdom.

John wrote the most detailed description of what is referred to as the Passion of Christ—the week of the crucifixion and resurrection of Jesus. It comes from the Latin word *passionem* which means "suffering, enduring."[1]

My prayer is that in studying the passion week, our personal passion will be stirred. We will be moved to lift our eyes from tasks, homework, and all the stuff of life and seek His kingdom first (Matt. 6:33).

VOLUNTEER, NOT VICTIM

"The name Gethsemane means 'oil press." The olives from trees in the garden were pressed into oil, which is "a picture of suffering."[2]

READ JOHN 18:1-11 and answer the following questions:

Who accompanied Judas to the garden and what did they have in their possession?

What statement of identity did Jesus make three times in this encounter (vv. 5,6,8)?

What question did Jesus ask after telling Peter to put away his sword?

Jesus wasn't a victim of circumstance; He voluntarily surrendered to the hard parts of the Father's call. So far Jesus had eluded capture by the religious authorities. But Judas led them to this secluded spot. They brought weapons believing Jesus might try to slip away again. However, Jesus had nothing to hide. He had been protected from arrest previously because His time had not yet come. Now His time had arrived. He proceeded willingly to drink the cup of suffering.

When considering our own suffering, we don't have to fear, knowing Jesus has gone before us. We are not alone. He is well-acquainted with sorrow (Isa. 53:3) and knows everything we might experience (Heb. 4:15).

> **If you are currently experiencing some challenges, write a few words or phrases describing your difficulties below.**

"The drinking of a cup is often used in Scripture to illustrate experiencing suffering or sorrow" (Isa. 51:17; Jer. 25:15–28).[3]

Take a moment to acknowledge the pain in your life, but seek God's help in walking through your suffering. He will be with you to help you change or endure, all for His purpose. Plus, keep in mind, God will transform your current difficulties into glory (2 Cor. 4:17-18).

IMPERFECT LEADERS

READ JOHN 18:15-18,25-27 and write anything that stands out to you about Peter's denial.

We know from Luke's Gospel that Jesus healed the servant Malchus's ear, which was His last recorded miracle before the cross (Luke 22:51).

John set up a contrast for us. When questioned, Jesus said, "I AM" (vv. 5-8). But Peter kept saying, "I am not." Jesus stood up to His questioners and denied nothing. Peter cowered before his questioners and denied everything. Peter fought the wrong enemy with the wrong weapon, slept when he should have been praying, and talked when he should have been listening. Then he denied Jesus three times.

We'll see later that Jesus forgave and restored Peter and eventually lifted him into leadership (John 21). Peter made impulsive decisions, but he turned away from sin and turned back to God. Soon we will find him preaching to multitudes about the gospel of Christ (Acts 2:14-41). Thankfully, Christ's kingdom makes room for imperfect leaders. No matter what we've done in the past, God can use us if we turn from our sin and turn toward Him.

How have you seen God use imperfect leaders (including yourself)?

As we consider Peter, we can exhibit grace for our leaders. They're human, just like us. So they aren't always going to get it right. We can also show grace to ourselves. The enemy wants to drown us in shame, extinguish hope, and convince us to give in to further temptation. Instead, we can confess our sin, turn from it, and experience forgiveness, which inspires change and hope.

GOD'S KINGDOM

READ JOHN 18:12-14,19-24,28-40 and list the people involved in leading Jesus's trials. Note how they are described and the actions they took.

VERSES	PERSON	DESCRIPTION/ACTIONS
Verses 13,24		

VERSES	PERSON	DESCRIPTION/ACTIONS
Verses 14,28		
Verses 29,33-40		

What stood out to you from Jesus's dialogue with those questioning Him?

I couldn't help but notice some huge contrasts between earthly kingdoms and Jesus's greater kingdom.

1. Caiaphas said it would be better for one man to die for the people (John 11:50; 18:14).

    - *Earthly kingdom:* Caiaphas was saying it would be better to kill one man to quell the disturbance than let it go on and the Roman government destroy the nation.

    - *Greater kingdom:* One man, Jesus, died for all, to pay the price for their sins.

2. Jesus's accusers didn't want to go inside the headquarters of the Roman government because they didn't want to defile themselves before Passover (18:28).

    - *Earthly kingdom:* Jews took precautions to avoid contamination in order to eat the Passover, while at the same time manipulating the judicial system to kill an innocent man.

    - *Greater kingdom:* Jesus is the ultimate Passover lamb who takes away the sin of the world.

3. The people asked for the criminal Barabbas to be released rather than Jesus (18:38-40).

    - *Earthly kingdom:* Barabbas's name means "son of a father."[4]

    - *Greater kingdom:* Jesus is the Son of the Father.

Individuals concerned with earthly kingdoms stressed over temporary problems. Jesus's greater kingdom was concerned with eternal restoration. Jesus taught about a reverse economy that values service, humility, forgiveness, and love.

Let's take a moment to check our own hearts. Where have earthly concerns overshadowed Jesus's kingdom priorities in your life lately?

Peter showed us that no matter how far we've gotten off track, we can be restored and walk in a new direction.

STOP AND SAVOR

Today we focused on this truth: *We can spend less time stressing over earthly pursuits when we remember that Jesus's kingdom is not of this world.*

What's one thing you hope to remember about what you studied today?

How does Peter's restoration encourage you?

PRAYER

Lord, you are the great I AM. You spoke the truth and you are the truth. Help me not to get so bogged down in the stuff of this world that I forget about your kingdom. I don't want to elevate the world's values above yours. Help me hold onto your kingdom priorities of love, truth, and forgiveness today! In Jesus's name, Amen.

Day Two
A PASSIONATE PRICE

I look back on times of my life where I wish I would've done things differently. Do you have stories you'd like to rewrite? Maybe you would be less angry, set better boundaries, or establish better habits. We have an enemy who loves to remind us of past sins and failures in hopes that guilt would drive us to despair.

As we read the account of Jesus's death on the cross, we don't want to merely feel sad for what He suffered. We don't just contemplate the cross—we carry it with us, savoring these gospel truths and believing that His death brings us life today and every day. Everything you feel guilty about today was wiped out two thousand years ago on the cross!

Today, we will connect Old Testament prophecy with its New Testament fulfillment to see that Jesus offered Himself as the perfect Passover lamb to remove our guilt.

THE SILENT LAMB

READ JOHN 19:1-16 and answer the following questions:

How was Jesus treated (vv. 1-3)?

What did the Jewish leaders state as Jesus's offense (v. 7)?

What emotion did Pilate express when he heard the charge against Jesus (v. 8)?

SCRIPTURE FOCUS
John 19

BIG IDEA
Jesus offered Himself as the perfect Passover lamb to remove our guilt.

The crown of thorns was possibly made "from the branches of the thorny acanthus shrub or from the date palm."[5]

Summarize what Jesus said when He finally spoke to Pilate (v. 11).

Jesus didn't answer Pilate's questions or defend Himself. He fulfilled prophecy with His silence.

> He was oppressed and treated harshly, yet he never said a word. He was led like a lamb to the slaughter. And as a sheep is silent before the shearers, he did not open his mouth.
>
> ISAIAH 53:7

When we consider the severity of the beating Jesus took, His silence in the face of such grave injustice feels even more compelling. Roman soldiers used a whip made of leather thongs with pieces of bone or metal attached, and typically only stopped from their own exhaustion or when an officer in authority commanded it.[6]

As I reflect on this passage, I'm moved knowing that what Jesus endured was meant for me. He carried it for me, for us. I'm also struck by Jesus's firm trust in God's sovereignty even as He was mocked and beaten. It reminds us that no power can touch us except what is allowed from above.

What stands out to you after reading these verses?

THE ROYAL LAMB

READ JOHN 19:17-27 and then read the following Old Testament prophecies. Write the verse number in John that fulfills each prophecy:

VERSE IN JOHN 19	OLD TESTAMENT PROPHECY
	I will give him the honors of a victorious soldier, because he exposed himself to death. He was counted among the rebels. He bore the sins of many and interceded for rebels. (*Isaiah 53:12*)

VERSE IN JOHN 19	OLD TESTAMENT PROPHECY
	They divide my garments among themselves and throw dice for my clothing. (*Psalm 22:18*)

Historical descriptions of the crucifixion vary slightly. One scholar describes Jesus laying down on the cross where His arms and legs were nailed and then hoisted up a piece of wood that served as a kind of seat which partially supported His weight. This wasn't designed to relieve agony but to increase it.[7] "To breathe, it was necessary to push with the legs and pull with the arms to keep the chest cavity open and functioning. Terrible muscle spasm wracked the entire body; but since collapse meant asphyxiation, the strain went on and on."[8]

In the midst of this terrible agony, Jesus spoke tenderly to His mother. Likely four women stood watching: Jesus's mother, her sister, Mary the wife of Clopas, and Mary Magdalene.[9] Jesus wanted to be sure His mother was cared for and assigned John, the writer of the Gospel, to meet her needs.

In the Roman world of Jesus's day, the language they spoke was Aramaic, the official language of the empire was Latin, and the language common for communication was Greek.[10]

THE FINAL LAMB

READ JOHN 19:28-37 and again write the verse number(s) that corresponds with fulfilled prophecy:

VERSE NUMBER(S)	OLD TESTAMENT PROPHECY
	But instead, they give me poison for food; they offer me sour wine for my thirst. (*Psalm 69:21*)
	For the Lord protects the bones of the righteous; not one of them is broken! (*Psalm 34:20*) Each Passover lamb must be eaten in one house. Do not carry any of its meat outside, and do not break any of its bones. (*Exodus 12:46*)
	Then I will pour out a spirit of grace and prayer on the family of David and on the people of Jerusalem. They will look on me whom they have pierced and mourn for him as for an only son. They will grieve bitterly for him as for a firstborn son who has died. (*Zechariah 12:10*)

The sour wine Jesus asked for fulfilled prophecy and was also meant to moisten Jesus's lips so He could speak loudly enough for the crowd to hear His final words.[12]

After drinking the cup of suffering, Jesus cried out *tetelestai*, a Greek expression that means, "it is finished." This was no cry of defeat or announcement of impending death. *Tetelestai* was an expression used in everyday life: a servant letting a master know he had finished a task, an artist or writer finishing a project, a merchant declaring a debt was paid in full, or a priest declaring an animal sacrifice faultless.[11]

Jesus had completed all the Father asked of Him.

Jesus was the perfect Lamb of God whom John the Baptist identified early in John's Gospel:

> The next day John saw Jesus coming toward him and said, "Look! The Lamb of God who takes away the sin of the world! He is the one I was talking about when I said, 'A man is coming after me who is far greater than I am, for he existed long before me.'"
> JOHN 1:29-30

Jesus's death declared our sin debt is paid in full. We can live without guilt because Jesus purchased our forgiveness through His shed blood.

How does reading the details of Jesus's sacrifice bring new appreciation for the price of your forgiveness?

As I consider that question, I feel grateful. I can savor peace today because Jesus endured the cross for me. I may still feel conviction when I sin, but the weight of guilt is gone.

BURIAL OF THE LAMB

READ JOHN 19:38-42 and identify the two men who were responsible for Jesus's burial.

1.

2.

We know little about Joseph of Arimathea apart from his involvement in securing permission and a place for Christ's burial. John is the only gospel writer who includes the detail about Nicodemus's participation. As men familiar with the law, both Joseph and Nicodemus likely recognized the prophecy we've explored today and believed that Jesus fulfilled the Passover as the slain Lamb of God.

His shed blood covers us from the penalty of sin. We have life through His sacrifice. While we don't savor that Jesus suffered, we can savor all that His suffering accomplished.

STOP AND SAVOR

Today we focused on this truth: *Jesus offered Himself as the perfect Passover lamb to remove our guilt.*

What's one thing you hope to remember about what you studied today?

How does this story, which is anything but peaceful, bring us peace?

What guilt do you need to leave at the foot of the cross today?

The seventy-five pounds of spices were worth a hundred years' wages. "The extravagance underlines the devotion of these formerly secret believers."[13]

PRAYER

Jesus, thank you for willingly enduring the cross for me. I'm so grateful that I don't have to live with guilt and shame. Help me to remember the passionate price you paid to remove my guilt and secure my peace with God. You are the messiah, the Lamb of God who takes away my sin! In Jesus's name, Amen.

Day Three
PASSIONATE PEACE

BIG IDEA

We can move toward greater faith as we review the first followers' responses to the empty tomb.

I remember sitting on a bus in middle school, staring out the window and reasoning with God about His existence. My twelve-year-old brain wondered if I would have believed in a different religion if I'd been born in another region of the world. I asked God to help me know if He was truly the real God of the universe. It was the reasoning of a preteen wanting to know if God was real and worth spending my life following.

Since then, I have studied God's Word and many belief systems of other faiths. One event has deepened my faith like nothing else. If John's Gospel had ended at chapter 19, Jesus would have been an exceptional character who made extraordinary claims. What sets Jesus apart from every other religious or moral teacher is His empty tomb.

The apostle Paul wrote a letter to the church at Corinth referencing the resurrection this way: "And if Christ has not been raised, then all our preaching is useless, and your faith is useless" (1 Cor. 15:14). As we read John 20 today, I pray we will move toward greater faith as we review the first followers' responses to the empty tomb.

PETER AND JOHN RUNNING

READ JOHN 20:1-10 and order the following events, 1 to 6.

_____ Peter arrived at the tomb and immediately went in.

_____ Mary found the stone rolled away from the tomb.

_____ Peter and the beloved disciple both ran to the tomb.

_____ The beloved disciple entered the tomb and believed that Jesus rose from the dead.

_____ Mary ran and told two disciples that Jesus's body was not in the tomb.

_____ The beloved disciple outran Peter but did not go into the tomb.

As a reminder, who is the beloved disciple?

we know from the other Gospel accounts that multiple women were going to the tomb along with Mary to finish anointing Jesus with spices.[14]

Remember that John never referred to himself by name in his Gospel—always "the one whom Jesus loved." It cracks me up that he included his victory over Peter in the footrace to the tomb (v. 4). Throughout John's Gospel, Jesus's pace had been slow and deliberate. Now the disciples were running, motivated by powerful emotions as they processed Jesus's death.

MARY CRYING

READ JOHN 20:11-18. What convinced Mary the man she was speaking to was Jesus?

Jesus first appeared in bodily form to a crying woman. When Mary heard her name, she knew it was the Lord. She likely prostrated herself at Jesus's feet and held onto Him (Matt. 28:9). Jesus then sent her to declare His appearance to His "brothers" (John 20:17), referring to His disciples. When Jesus mentioned "my Father and your Father, to my God and your God," He was including Mary in the kingdom family with His language.[15]

Jesus rose for Mary, and for you and me. Believing in Him brings us into the same kingdom family. Whether this week has included running toward Jesus or crying in confusion, we can rest our faith on the fact that Jesus is alive!

In the culture of Jesus's day, a woman's testimony was not valued or seen as credible. That validates John's reporting that Jesus first appeared to a woman, Mary Magdalene. It also shows how Jesus's values were far different from His culture.[16]

THE DISCIPLES FEARING

READ JOHN 20:19-23 and write the repeated phrase Jesus spoke to His disciples in verses 19 and 21.

The disciples met in a room with locked doors because they feared the Jewish leaders. After He repeated the peace greeting, He then:

- Sent them out as the Father had sent Him. They were not to stay huddled up behind closed doors but to go into all the world with the gospel.

- Breathed on them to receive the Holy Spirit. Scholars debate what this means in light of Acts 2. Some say it was a temporary filling while others say it was a spiritual endowment, preparing them for what would take place at Pentecost.[17]

- Highlighted that forgiveness was at the center of their message. They wouldn't have power and authority to forgive, but they would have the power and authority to proclaim forgiveness found in Christ.[18]

Jesus commissioned the disciples in the midst of their fears. We face our own brand of fear. Maybe our finances, health, or relationships have us locking the doors of our hearts. But Jesus speaks peace over us in the midst of troubling circumstances and sends us out in the power of the Holy Spirit with the message of forgiveness. We don't need to wait until we're fear-free to follow Jesus.

How has the peace of Jesus freed you to serve and share even in the midst of your current challenges?

THOMAS DOUBTING

READ JOHN 20:24-29 and describe in your own words Jesus's response to Thomas.

Clearly Thomas hadn't totally abandoned his faith because he continued to meet with the disciples. Jesus knew Thomas's struggle and didn't shame him. Instead, Jesus provided what Thomas needed to move from doubt to faith.

This encounter reminds us that we can press into our doubts with Christ, exploring, asking questions, and genuinely seeking truth.

How does Thomas's experience encourage you when it comes to doubts, whether your own or those experienced by people in your circle of influence?

YOU AND I BELIEVING

READ JOHN 20:30-31 and fill in the blanks below:

"But these are written so that you may continue to _____ that Jesus is the Messiah, the Son of God, and that by believing in him you will have _____ by the power of his name" (John 20:31, NLT).

John made clear his purpose in recording this account of Jesus's life, death, and resurrection—so we might believe in Him and have life in His name. Hallelujah!

STOP AND SAVOR

Today we focused on this truth: *We can move toward greater faith as we review the first followers' responses to the empty tomb.*

What's one thing you hope to remember about what you studied today?

How has Jesus met you personally in your confusion, fear, heartbreak, or doubt?

PRAYER

Jesus, I know you are the Son of God. You died, but you rose from the dead. When I run, help me to run toward you. When I'm sad, help me to bring my sadness to you. When I'm afraid, help me to find peace in you. When I'm doubting, helping me to work through my questions with you. Fill me with your Holy Spirit so I can proclaim the gospel and serve others in your love. In Jesus's name, Amen.

Session Seven: Peace in the Passion of Jesus   163

Day Four

PASSION FOR PEOPLE

**SCRIPTURE
FOCUS**

John 21:1–24

BIG IDEA

*Vertical love for
Jesus propels us
toward horizontal
care for others.*

Social media helps me keep up with old friends, hear inspiration from
Bible teachers, and laugh at amusing videos. However, I can also get
sidetracked by advertised products or find myself coveting other peoples'
vacations, accomplishments, or seemingly uncomplicated lives. Sometimes
looking sideways at others' lives prevents me from looking up at Jesus.

In what ways do you find yourself similarly distracted?

FUTILE FISHING

READ JOHN 21:1-3. How long did they fish and
what did they catch?

*On the Sea of
Galilee, nighttime
is reported to be
the time for more
productive fishing.
The catch could then
be brought in and
sold in the morning.[19]*

The disciples knew Jesus was alive and had promised them His Spirit.
They waited at the Sea of Galilee (also called the Sea of Tiberius), likely
because Jesus told them He would meet them in Galilee (Matt. 28:7;
Mark 16:7). Peter announced that he was going fishing and the others
followed his lead. His motivation to head out to sea is not given in the
text. Maybe he got restless. I can relate. Often, we revert to familiar
routines when we lack direction. Sitting tight is difficult. But when we
move without divine inspiration, we often end up with only perspiration
to show for it.

**When have you struggled to know what came next
in God's plan? How did you deal with being unsure
where to go or what to do?**

The disciples didn't have to wait long. Jesus showed up with encouragement and direction. In His time, He will provide clarity for you, too!

FAITH FISHING

READ JOHN 21:4-14 and draw a line from the person to the action or statement. (Some people will be used more than once.)

He told the disciples to throw their nets on the right side of the boat.

He said, "It is the Lord!"

He put on his tunic and jumped in the water.

He dragged the fish-filled net to shore.

He invited the disciples to eat breakfast.

Jesus

Peter

John, the beloved disciple

When Jesus directed their fishing, the disciples pulled in "153 large fish" (v. 11). It's pure speculation to see any significance to the number. John probably included the detail because it was such a large amount. What we can know from this number is that things get exciting when Jesus shows up! When we follow His instructions by faith, we can accomplish exponentially more than what is humanly possible.

Seasons of waiting can cause us to hyperfocus on natural methods to discern God's direction, like pros and cons lists, spreadsheets, or Google® searches. These aren't necessarily harmful practices as long as we are looking up more than sideways for guidance.

SHEPHERDING SHEEP

READ JOHN 21:15-17 and fill in the chart with the missing information. (Answers will vary depending on translation.)

VERSE	JESUS'S QUESTION	PETER'S ANSWER	JESUS'S RESPONSE
Verse 15	Do you love me more than these?		Feed my lambs.

Verse 16		Yes, Lord. You know I love You.	Take care of my sheep.
Verse 17	Do you love me?		

Two different Greek words for "love" are used in this passage: *agapao*—divine love (Jesus's first two questions) and *phileo*—brotherly love (Jesus's third question and Peter's three replies).[20] However, the consensus among commentators is that we shouldn't read too much into the word variance, especially since the original conversation likely took place in Aramaic.[21] John's Greek word choice likely had more to do with his writing style than disclosing a hidden meaning about types of love.[22]

Peter had previously made some pretty bold boasts (John 13:37, Matt. 26:33,35). But in this moment, instead of bragging, Peter was broken. He had grossly overestimated his abilities. I can't help but put myself in Peter's shoes.

How have you experienced humility on the other side of failure?

I'm feeling it today. I woke up discouraged at 4:00 a.m. and couldn't get back to sleep. I slipped out of bed and began journaling. I told the Lord everything He already knew and experienced His grace once again. Today I feel especially grateful for Peter's commissioning to feed God's sheep. The Lord doesn't write us off when we fail. He will continue to call us and use us when we turn back to Him in faith.

CARING INSTEAD OF COMPARING

READ JOHN 21:18-24 and write Peter's question in verse 21.

Have you been asking some version of that question as you compare your situation to others? You don't have to write anything; just consider whether you're distracted from keeping your eyes up toward God because you've been focused sideways on those around you.

Maybe you wish you had her health, his job, their ministry, or something else. When Jesus told Peter that imprisonment and death lay ahead for him, Peter turned around and asked about John. Jesus redirected Peter to leave other peoples' callings to Him. This truth is easier to read, study, and discuss than to live out.

Where is the Lord challenging you to keep your eyes on Him and away from comparative living?

What practices help you to fix your eyes on Christ?

Rather than measure the trials and blessings of others, we must keep our eyes on Jesus and seek God's glory in His call for us.

STOP AND SAVOR

Today we focused on this truth: *Vertical love for Jesus propels us toward horizontal care for others.*

What's one thing you hope to remember about what you studied today?

How does Jesus's interaction with Peter help you savor His peace?

According to church tradition, Peter was crucified upside down, probably in Rome during the reign of emperor Nero.[23]

> **PRAYER**
>
> Jesus, help me to wait for your directions rather than spinning my wheels in futility. Thank you for showing up with abundance and guiding my efforts. Lord, thank you for restoring Peter. His story reminds me that you are restoring me on the other side of my failures. Help me to keep my eyes fixed on you so I can care for those around me without comparison. In Jesus's name, Amen.

Day Five
MORE PASSION

As I reflect on my own journey through John, I recognize God's kindness toward me. He knew I would be walking through my dad's cancer and death during this season. Savoring the peace of Jesus in a chaotic world has been a gracious gift in my life during this time.

> **How have you experienced God's kindness during your study of John?**

Today we finish this Gospel and reflect on the impact of Jesus's message in our lives.

PEACE BEYOND OUR UNDERSTANDING

READ JOHN 21:25 and summarize the final verse.

John reminded us that Jesus's ministry could not be captured in one volume, four Gospel accounts, or any number of books. He is the Logos, the Living Word, whose love for His Father and His creation runs deeper than we can wrap our minds or words around. In his letter to the church at Philippi, the apostle Paul confirmed that we can't fully grasp the extent of what God has given us in Christ:

> Then you will experience God's peace, which exceeds anything we can understand. His peace will guard your hearts and minds as you live in Christ Jesus.
> **PHILIPPIANS 4:7**

The gospel of Jesus can't be explained nor contained in any one book, and the peace of Jesus exceeds our understanding! Both overdeliver because of God's kindness toward us.

PEACE IN THE CHAOS

Jesus assured us that in this world, we would have trouble (John 16:33). He tabernacled among us in human form so He felt that trouble personally (1:14). He cried when Lazarus died (11:35). He got angry over abuses in the temple (2:15). He grew weary (4:6). He saw the chaos we experience firsthand. Yet He reminded us that trouble doesn't get the final word.

READ AGAIN these words of Jesus and put a star next to the verses that stand out to you today.

John 3:16

John 10:10

John 14:1

John 14:27

John 16:33

When Jesus appeared to His disciples after the resurrection, He approached them with the words, "Peace be with you" (John 20:19,21). He speaks peace to us as well. He's not offering the absence of conflict, but a calm state of the soul in His presence.

Thank you for journeying with me through the pages of John. I pray that God's peace will continue to exceed our comprehension in the weeks and months ahead as we savor Jesus above all else in this chaotic world.

STOP AND SAVOR

Today we focused on this truth: *We can savor the peace of Jesus in a chaotic world.*

What are one or two personal takeaways from this study that you want to remember for the days, months, and years to come?

PRAYER

Jesus, you are my peace. Thank you for John's Gospel. Thank you for inviting me to come and spend time with you, Living Water and the Bread of Life. Help me not to forget what I've read and learned. I don't want to take your gift of peace for granted. Allow it to permeate my heart and my mind. Today, I'm savoring your peace, and I'm grateful that you were so passionate about me that you were willing to pay the highest price. In Jesus's name, Amen.

BEGIN

What is your favorite form of distraction (social media, gaming, binge watching your favorite show, etc.)?

Circle the emotion that best describes how you feel about your time with God this week. Share your answer with the group.

Happy   Content   Anxious   Sad   Angry

If you could use any color to describe how you feel about life in general right now, what would it be? Why?

Review the big ideas from this session. Which one did you enjoy the most? If any, which one did you struggle to relate to?

Based on your study from John 18–21, what are two qualities of Jesus that stand out to you?

As a group, review your memory verse from this session (John 20:31).

Choose one person to pray over the group and for your discussion time, that it would be beneficial for everyone and honoring to God.

REVIEW & DISCUSS

Take some time to thoughtfully review what you've learned over the course of the study and discuss each reflection question.

SESSION TITLE	REFLECT
Peace in the Plan of Jesus John 1–3	As you consider God's unfailing plan to save His people, what plans can you surrender to Him today?
Peace in the Power of Jesus John 4–6	As you reflect on the seven signs John highlighted, what are you boldly asking God to do in your life? (See margin to review signs.)
Peace in the Patience of Jesus John 7–9	Where is the Lord calling you to look beneath the surface, so you can judge correctly in a current situation?
Peace in the Purposes of Jesus John 10–13	How have you experienced God's abundance in a specific way over the course of our time together?
Peace in the Promises of Jesus John 14–17	How has the Holy Spirit been your Advocate, defending, comforting, and strengthening you?
Peace in the Passion of Jesus John 18–21	Jesus's passion for you took Him all the way to the cross. Spend a few moments thanking Him for His love.

The seven signs Jesus performed in John include water to wine, healing an official's son, healing a man by the pool, feeding of the five thousand, walking on water, healing a man born blind, and raising Lazarus.

REFLECT & APPLY

Check out the following names and descriptions of Jesus that are found in John's Gospel. Circle a few you have savored during this study:

water-walker	True Vine	Logos, Living Word
Way, Truth, Life	Living Water	Creator
Lamb of God	Bread of Life	Healer
Messiah	Son of God	Son of Man
Generous Host	Noticer	Rabbi (Teacher)
Patient	Peace	Light of the world
The Door	Resurrection and Life	

Share one of the names/descriptions you circled and why. If something from the study stood out to you about Jesus that isn't listed above, feel free to add it.

What are some practical ways to maintain the habit of stopping and savoring Jesus after this study is over?

In your final "Stop and Savor," you were asked to write down one or two takeaways from the study that you want to remember. Share your answers with the group.

How many of the memory verses can you recite today? Which one has meant the most to you during these sessions?

CLOSE

Use the journaling space below (or a separate journal) to write out a personal prayer to Jesus as you reflect on finishing this Bible study. Give Him praise for all the ways He has revealed Himself to you over these seven sessions, then pour your heart out to Him. Write down what's on your mind, how you're struggling, if you have questions, where you still want peace. Invite His presence to be near.

leader guide

TIPS FOR LEADING A GROUP

Pray diligently. Ask God to prepare you to lead this study. Pray individually and specifically for the girls in your group. Make this a priority in your personal walk and preparation.

Prepare adequately. Don't just wing this. Take time to preview each week so you have a good grasp of the content. Look over the group session and consider those in your group. Feel free to delete or reword the questions provided, and add questions that fit your group better.

Lead by example. Make sure you complete all of the personal study. Be willing to share your story, what you're learning, and your questions as you discuss together.

Be aware. If girls are hesitant to discuss their thoughts and questions in a larger group, consider dividing into smaller groups to provide a setting more conducive to conversation.

Follow up. If someone mentions a prayer request or need, make sure to follow up. It may be a situation where you can get others in the group involved in helping out.

Evaluate often. After each week and throughout the study, assess what needs to be changed to more effectively lead the study.

SCAN THE QR CODE TO FIND SOCIAL ASSETS AND ADDITIONAL LEADER RESOURCES.

MAKE THE MOST OF YOUR GROUP TIME

If you are leading a Bible study group through *The Gospel of John*, then first I want to say thank you! I have no doubt God will use you to encourage the girls in your group as you walk through His Word together. I can't wait to get started on this journey alongside you. I'm excited to slow down and linger with Jesus to receive the gift of peace He promised. I pray you'll join me in the pages of John's Gospel, and we can grow in our faith, find life, and savor peace together.

BEGIN

Help ease into each session by starting off with some questions to get girls comfortable with one another. This opening section is also the perfect time to break out the snacks and some comfy seating options. After Session One, this will be a great time to reflect on what they learned and review the memory verse for the week.

REVIEW & DISCUSS

At your first group meeting, watch the Session One video together, discuss the questions provided, and make sure all the girls in your group have their Bible study book. When you gather for Session Two, you'll discuss what you studied during the week and then watch the Session Two video together. It will be extremely helpful for you, as the leader, to watch the videos and read through the questions ahead of Group Time to prepare for discussion.

REFLECT & APPLY

These questions and Scripture references are designed to bring deeper discussion. You are more than welcome to ask additional questions that you feel are important, or you can skip the questions we provided if your girls are owning the discussion with their own notes from the personal study. Bottom line: follow the Holy Spirit's leading as you enter into this time.

CLOSE

Before you end your time together, you will want to go over the memory verse and personal study they should focus on before you meet next. Then, close out in prayer using the prayer practice as a way to encourage your girls before they are dismissed.

mom & daughter guide

Mom, we are so excited that you have decided to complete this study with your daughter. As Melissa Spoelstra walks you through the book of John, you will find an invitation for both you and your daughter to slow down, to linger with the Word of God, and to savor the peace of Christ.

YOU WILL NEED

The Gospel of John: Women's Bible Study Book for yourself

The Gospel of John: Teen Girls' Bible Study Book for your daughter(s)

VIDEO CONTENT

The weekly videos that are included in the women's Bible study book can be watched with your daughter during the Group Time sessions. Follow the instructions in the back of your women's Bible study book to access the teaching videos. Note: the videos included in the teen girl Bible study book are the introduction videos only to allow more time for discussion.

STUDY

At the close of each session, you will spend time working through the Group Time found in the *The Gospel of John: Teen Girls' Bible Study Book*. The discussion questions will help you go deeper as you review your personal study and share what you've learned each week.

As you both work through your individual Bible study books, you will discover that the teen girls' version might be slightly different as we altered some language and content to be more applicable for teen girls. However, there are very few differences in the studies, and we encourage you to discuss what the Lord is teaching you individually.

CONNECT WITH HER

Plan days to work on personal study together to keep each other accountable. Be open with your daughter throughout the week about things you learn or have questions about. Provide a safe place for her to do the same. Don't stress! Some weeks will be easier than others to accomplish the personal study days. Just keep pressing forward and making it a priority to meet together each week regardless of how much personal study work was actually done.

FAQ

Q: How old does my teen need to be for this study?

A: This study is recommended for girls ages 11 and up.

Q: Are there other studies I can do with my daughter after this study is over?

A: Yes! Many of our studies have both women's and teen girls' materials available. Check it out at lifeway.com/girls.

Read Through John

**SESSION ONE:
INTRODUCTION
TO THIS STUDY**

**SESSION TWO: PEACE
IN THE PLAN OF JESUS**
- ☐ Day One: John 1:1-34
- ☐ Day Two: John 1:35-51
- ☐ Day Three: John 2:1-22
- ☐ Day Four: John 2:23–3:21
- ☐ Day Five: John 3:22-36

**SESSION THREE: PEACE
IN THE POWER OF JESUS**
- ☐ Day One: John 4:1-42
- ☐ Day Two: John 4:43–5:15
- ☐ Day Three: John 5:16-45
- ☐ Day Four: John 6:1-21
- ☐ Day Five: John 6:22-71

**SESSION FOUR: PEACE IN
THE PATIENCE OF JESUS**
- ☐ Day One: John 7:1-36
- ☐ Day Two: John 7:37-52
- ☐ Day Three: John 8:1-11
- ☐ Day Four: John 8:12-59
- ☐ Day Five: John 9

**SESSION FIVE: PEACE IN
THE PURPOSES OF JESUS**
- ☐ Day One: John 10
- ☐ Day Two: John 11
- ☐ Day Three: John 12
- ☐ Day Four: John 13:1-17
- ☐ Day Five: John 13:18-35

**SESSION SIX: PEACE IN
THE PROMISES OF JESUS**
- ☐ Day One: John 14:1-14
- ☐ Day Two: John 14:15-31
- ☐ Day Three: John 15
- ☐ Day Four: John 16
- ☐ Day Five: John 17

**SESSION SEVEN: PEACE IN
THE PASSION OF JESUS**
- ☐ Day One: John 18
- ☐ Day Two: John 19
- ☐ Day Three: John 20
- ☐ Day Four: John 21:1-24
- ☐ Day Five: John 21:25

HOW TO BECOME A CHRISTIAN

Romans 10:17 says, "So faith comes from what is heard, and what is heard comes through the message about Christ."

Maybe you've stumbled across new information in this study. Or maybe you've attended church all your life, but something you read here struck you differently than it ever has before. If you have never accepted Christ but would like to, read on to discover how you can become a Christian.

Your heart tends to run from God and rebel against Him. The Bible calls this sin. Romans 3:23 says, "For everyone has sinned; we all fall short of God's glorious standard."

Yet God loves you and wants to save you from sin, to offer you a new life of hope. John 10:10b says, "My purpose is to give them a rich and satisfying life."

To give you this gift of salvation, God made a way through His Son, Jesus Christ. Romans 5:8 says, "But God showed his great love for us by sending Christ to die for us while we were still sinners."

You receive this gift by faith alone. Ephesians 2:8-9 says, "God saved you by his grace when you believed. And you can't take credit for this; it is a gift from God. Salvation is not a reward for the good things we have done, so none of us can boast about it."

Faith is a decision of your heart demonstrated by the actions of your life. Romans 10:9 says, "If you openly declare that Jesus is Lord and believe in your heart that God raised him from the dead, you will be saved."

If you trust that Jesus died for your sins and want to receive new life through Him, pray a prayer similar to the following to express your repentance and faith in Him:

Dear God, I know I am a sinner. I believe Jesus died to forgive me of my sins. I accept Your offer of eternal life. Thank You for forgiving me of all my sins. Thank You for my new life. From this day forward, I will choose to follow You.

If you have trusted Jesus for salvation, please share your decision with your group leader or another Christian friend. If you are not already attending church, find one in which you can worship and grow in your faith. Following Christ's example, ask to be baptized as a public expression of your faith.

Timeline
FOR THE GOSPEL OF JOHN

26–36
Pontius Pilate is prefect of Judea

 AD 18–29

18–36
Caiaphas is high priest

Winter 32/33
Growing opposition to Jesus at the Festival of Dedication

32
Jesus's feeding of the five thousand during Passover

Autumn 32
Jesus's teachings at the Festival of Shelters

Winter 33
Jesus raises Lazarus from the dead

Nisan 9, 33 (March 29)
Jesus's triumphal entry into Jerusalem Sunday

AD 33

Late Winter 33
Jesus's teachings at the Festival of Shelters

Monday, Nisan 10, 33
Jesus's second cleansing of the temple

For a more detailed possible timeline of the Gospel of John, check out this website:
https://biblicalfoundations.org/johannine-chronology/

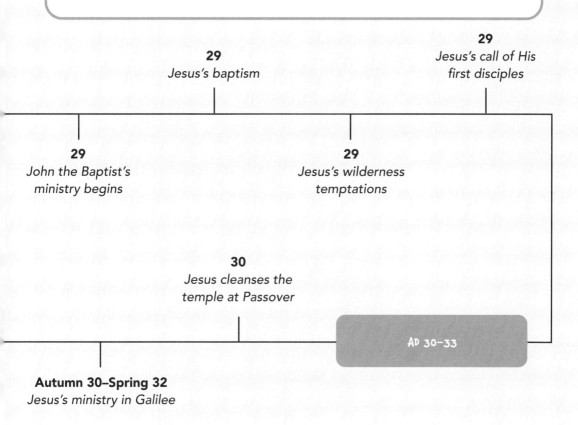

29
Jesus's baptism

29
Jesus's call of His
first disciples

29
John the Baptist's
ministry begins

29
Jesus's wilderness
temptations

30
Jesus cleanses the
temple at Passover

AD 30–33

Autumn 30–Spring 32
Jesus's ministry in Galilee

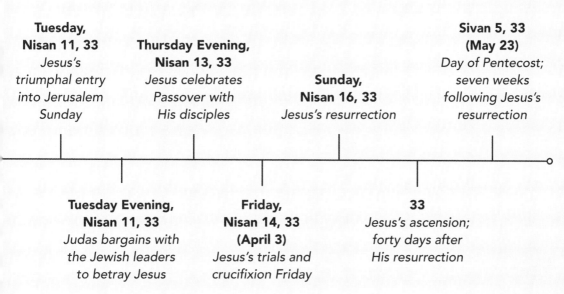

**Tuesday,
Nisan 11, 33**
Jesus's
triumphal entry
into Jerusalem
Sunday

**Thursday Evening,
Nisan 13, 33**
Jesus celebrates
Passover with
His disciples

**Sunday,
Nisan 16, 33**
Jesus's resurrection

**Sivan 5, 33
(May 23)**
Day of Pentecost;
seven weeks
following Jesus's
resurrection

**Tuesday Evening,
Nisan 11, 33**
Judas bargains with
the Jewish leaders
to betray Jesus

**Friday,
Nisan 14, 33
(April 3)**
Jesus's trials and
crucifixion Friday

33
Jesus's ascension;
forty days after
His resurrection

MAPS DURING THE TIME OF JOHN

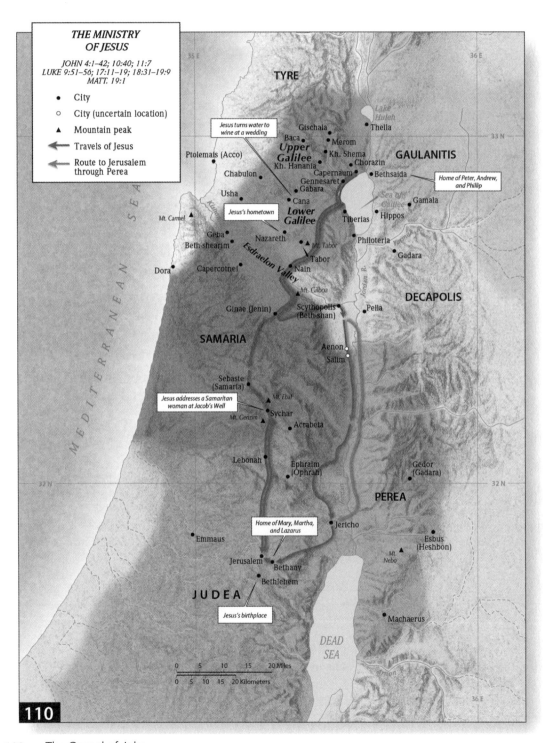

THE MINISTRY OF JESUS

JOHN 4:1–42; 10:40; 11:7
LUKE 9:51–56; 17:11–19; 18:31–19:9
MATT. 19:1

- • City
- ○ City (uncertain location)
- ▲ Mountain peak
- ← Travels of Jesus
- ← Route to Jerusalem through Perea

TYRE

Lake Huleh

Gischala · Thella

Baca · Merom

Upper Galilee · Kh. Shema

Ptolemais (Acco) · Kh. Hanania · Chorazin

GAULANITIS

Chabulon · Capernaum · Bethsaida

Home of Peter, Andrew, and Phillip

Gennesaret

Usha · Gabara

Cana · Sea of Galilee · Gamala

Lower Galilee · Tiberias · Hippos

Mt. Carmel ▲ *Jesus's hometown*

Geba · Nazareth · Mt. Tabor ▲ · Philoteria

Beth-shearim · Tabor · Gadara

Esdraelon Valley

Dora · Capercotnei · Nain

Mt. Gilboa ▲

DECAPOLIS

Ginae (Jenin) · Scythopolis (Beth-shan) · Pella

SAMARIA

Aenon ○ · Salim

Sebaste (Samaria)

Jesus addresses a Samaritan woman at Jacob's Well

Mt. Ebal ▲ · Sychar

Mt. Gerizim ▲ · Acrabeta

Lebonah · Ephraim (Ophrah)

Gedor (Gadara)

PEREA

Home of Mary, Martha, and Lazarus · Jericho

Emmaus · Esbus (Heshbon)

Mt. Nebo ▲

Jerusalem · Bethany

Bethlehem

JUDEA

Jesus's birthplace · Machaerus

DEAD SEA

Jesus turns water to wine at a wedding

MEDITERRANEAN SEA

Kishon

Jordan R.

0   5   10   15   20 Miles
0   5   10   15   20 Kilometers

35 E · 36 E · 33 N · 32 N · 32 N · 36 E

110

JERUSALEM IN THE
NEW TESTAMENT PERIOD

][Gate
— Tower
▪▪▪▪▪ Wall
x Spot elevation
-2400- Contour interval = 33ft. (10m)

Josephus' Third North Wall

Tower of Psephinus

Golgotha
(Gordon's Calvary)   x 2548

Josephus' Second North Wall

Bezetha

Fish Gate

Antonia Fortress

Jesus healed a
paralytic man in
the Pool of Bethesda

Mt. of Olives

x 2445

Judgement Gate

Jesus crucified
on Golgotha

Golgotha
(traditional location)

Tyropoeon Valley

Wilson's Arch
(bridge)

Temple Mount
Warren's Gate
Altar

Sheep Gate

Gethsemane

Solomon's Portico
Shushan Gate
Beautiful Gate

x 2684

Kidron Valley

Tower of Hippicus

First N. Wall

Josephus'

Xystus?

Temple

Royal Portico

Jesus taught in
the temple
precincts

Tower of Phasael
Tower of Mariamne

Praetorium

Jesus on trial
here before
crucifixion

Herod's
Family
Tomb(s)

Upper City

Herod's Palace

x 2486 Herod
Gennath Antipas'
Gate palace
x 2532

Wealthy
residential
area

Theater

Barclay's Gate

Huldah Gates

Pinnacle of
Temple
(traditional
location)

Valley Gate

Robinson's
Arch
(stairs)

Lower City

House of Caiaphas,
the high priest

Essene
Quarter

Escarpment

City Of David

Gihon Spring

x 2437

Upper Room
(traditional location)

Essene Gate

Water Gate

Hinnom

0   1/8   1/4 Mile
0   150   300 Meters

MEDITERRANEAN SEA

34 E   35 E   36 E

33 N

32 N

Jerusalem

Area
enlarged
at left

DEAD
SEA

31 N

30 N

Notes

Notes

Notes

Notes

ENDNOTES

Session One

1. John F. Hart, "John," in *The Moody Bible Commentary,* ed. Michael A. Rydelnik and Michael Vanlaningham (Chicago, IL: Moody Publishers, 2014), 1605–1606.

2. *"Eirene,"* Bible Study Tools, accessed Sept. 8, 2023. Available at www.biblestudytools.com/lexicons/greek/nas/eirene.html.

Session Two

1. *The Expositor's Bible Commentary,* vol. 9, ed. Frank E. Gaebelein (Grand Rapids, MI: The Zondervan Corporation, 1981), 29.

2. Ibid.

3. Ibid., 40.

4. Ibid.

5. Ibid., 41.

6. R. C. Sproul, *John: An Expositional Commentary* (Sanford, FL: Ligonier Ministries, 2009), 20.

7. *Zondervan Illustrated Bible Backgrounds Commentary,* vol. 2A, eds., Craig S. Keener (Grand Rapids, MI: Zondervan, 2019), 21.

8. R. C. Sproul, "The Wedding at Cana," Ligonier Ministries, Jan. 19, 2018. Available at www.ligonier.org/learn/devotionals/wedding-at-cana.

9. Keener, 21. Also see Edward W. Klink III, *John: Exegetical Commentary on the New Testament* (Grand Rapids, MI: Zondervan Academic, 2016), 164.

10. Ibid.

11. Sproul, 22.

12. Keener, 23.

13. Warren W. Wiersbe, *Be Alive* (Colorado Springs, CO: David C Cook, 2009), 43.

14. *"Pisteuo,"* Bible Study Tools, accessed Oct. 16, 2023. Available at www.biblestudytools.com/lexicons/greek/nas/pisteuo.html.

15. Ibid.

16. Wiersbe, 52.

17. Sproul, 37.

18. Keener, 30.

19. Sproul, 44.

Session Three

1. Kenneth E. Bailey, *Jesus Through Middle Eastern Eyes* (Downers Grove, IL: InterVarsity Press, 2008), 201.

2. Ibid., 202.

3. Ibid., 203.

4. Ibid., 202.

5. Edward W. Klink III, *John: Exegetical Commentary on the New Testament* (Grand Rapids, MI: Zondervan Academic, 2016), 261.

6. Ibid., 271.

7. Weirsbe, 79.

8. Gerald L. Borchert, *The New American Commentary, John 1–11,* vol. 25A (Nashville, TN: Broadman & Holman Publishers, 1996). Accessed through Logos Bible Software. Available at www.logos.com.

9. "Eschatology," *Merriam-Webster's Dictionary,* accessed Oct. 16, 2023. Available at www.merriam-webster.com/dictionary/eschatology.

10. Wiersbe, 85.

11. Ibid., 86.

12. Warren W. Wiersbe, *Warren Wiersbe BE Bible Study Series,* Bible Gateway, accessed Oct. 17, 2023. Available at www.biblegateway.com/resources/wiersbe-be-bible-study/3-he-claimed-that-there-are-valid-witnesses-who.

13. Klink, 303.

14. Ibid., 304.

15. Ibid., 311.

16. Leon Morris, *The Gospel According to John* (Grand Rapids, MI: Wm. B. Eerdmans Publishing Co., 1989), 361.

17. *"Mathetes,"* Bible Study Tools, accessed Oct. 19, 2023. Available at www.biblestudytools.com/lexicons/greek/nas/mathetes.html.

Session Four

1. Keener, 66.
2. *"Skenoo,"* Bible Study Tools, accessed Sept. 5, 2023. Available at www.biblestudytools.com/lexicons/greek/nas/skenoo.html.
3. Klink, 357.
4. Eli Lizorkin-Eyzenberg, *The Jewish Gospel of John: Discovering Jesus, King of All Israel* (Lizorkin-Eyzenberg, 2015–2019), 119.
5. Matt Carter and Josh Wredberg, *Christ-Centered Exposition Commentary: Exalting Jesus in John* (Nashville, TN: B&H Publishing Group, 2017), 179.
6. Keener, 75.
7. Bailey, 229.
8. Ibid., 57, 233–235.
9. Sproul, 141.
10. Ibid.
11. Ibid.
12. "Surprising facts about phobias," Aruma, accessed Oct. 20, 2023. Available at www.aruma.com.au/about-us/blog/surprising-facts-about-phobias.
13. D. A. Carson, *The Gospel According to John* (Grand Rapids, MI: Wm. B. Eerdmans Publishing Company, 1991), 337.
14. Wiersbe, 126.
15. Gaebelein, 92.
16. Carson, 345.
17. Keener, 93.
18. Klink, 441.
19. Klink, 444.
20. Keener, 97.

Session Five

1. Keener, 101.
2. Morris, 501.
3. Ibid., 502.
4. Carson, 382.
5. Morris, 503.
6. *"Perissos,"* Bible Study Tools, accessed Oct. 20, 2023. Available at www.biblestudytools.com/lexicons/greek/nas/perissos.html.
7. Carson, 381.
8. Morris, 509.
9. Gaebelein, 118.
10. Ibid., 119.
11. Ibid.
12. Carson, 430.
13. Ibid., 429.
14. Ibid., 433.
15. Ibid., 437.
16. Alyssa Roat, "What Does Agape Love Really Mean in the Bible?" Christianity.com, accessed Oct. 20, 2023. Available at www.christianity.com/wiki/christian-terms/what-does-agape-love-really-mean-in-the-bible.html.
17. Morris, 625; Keener, 141.
18. Keener, 142.
19. John MacArthur, *The MacArthur New Testament, John 12–21* (Chicago: Moody Publishers, 2008). Accessed through Logos Bible Software. Available at www.logos.com.
20. Carson, 473.

Session Six

1. Gaebelein, 143.
2. Klink, 615.
3. Lizorkin, 193.
4. Chip Ingram, "How to Pray When Anxiety Knocks at Your Heart," *Living on the Edge*, accessed Oct. 21, 2023. Available at https://livingontheedge.org/2018/04/30/how-to-pray-when-anxiety-knocks-at-your-heart.
5. Sproul, 252.
6. Gaebelein, 146.

7. Warren W. Wiersbe, *Be Transformed, John 13–21* (Colorado Springs, CO: David C Cook, 1986), 41.

8. Carson, 498.

9. Ibid., "*Eirene*," Bible Study Tools.

10. "*Shalowm*," Biblestudytools.com, accessed Sept. 8, 2023. Available at www.biblestudytools.com.

11. Carson, 506.

12. "*Meno*," Biblestudytools.com, accessed Sept. 9, 2023. Available online at www.biblestudytools.com/lexicons/greek/nas/meno.html.

13. *The MacArthur New Testament, John 12–21.*

14. Morris, 716.

Session Seven

1. "*Passion* (n.)," Online Etymology Dictionary, accessed Oct. 20, 2023. Available online at www.etymonline.com/word/passion.

2. Wiersbe, 106.

3. Ibid., 111.

4. "Matthew 27:16," *Gill's Exposition of the Entire Bible,* Bible Hub, accessed Oct. 23, 2023. Available at https://biblehub.com/commentaries/matthew/27-16.htm.

5. Keener, 184.

6. Carson, 597; Morris, 790.

7. Carson, 608.

8. Ibid., 610.

9. Carson, 615; Gaebelein, 182.

10. Morris, 807.

11. Wiersbe, 140.

12. Morris, 814.

13. Keener, 197.

14. Sproul, 352.

15. J. Ramsey Michaels, T*he New International Commentary on the New Testament, The Gospel of John* (Grand Rapids, MI: William B. Eerdmans Publishing Company, 2010). Accessed through Logos Bible Software. Available at www.logos.com.

16. Keener, 204.

17. Gerald L. Borchert, *The New American Commentary, John 12–21,* vol. 25 (Nashville, TN: Broadman & Holman Publishers, 2002). Accessed through Logos Bible Software. Available at www.logos.com.

18. Kenneth O. Gangel, *Holman New Testament Commentary,* Max Anders, ed. (Nashville, TN: Broadman & Holman Publishers, 2000). Accessed through Logos Bible Software. Available at www.logos.com.

19. Keener, 208.

20. Gaebelein, 201.

21. Morris, 873.

22. Carson, 678; Wiersbe, 182; Keener, 211; Morris, 873.

23. Carson, 680; Wiersbe, 184; Keener, 212.

Lifeway girls

Helping you point girls to Christ

Social

@lifewaygirls

additional resources

Blog | girlsministry.lifeway.com

Shop | lifeway.com/girls

Podcast | His Glory, Her Good

Get the most from your study.

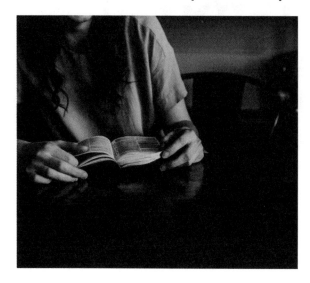

In this study you'll:

- Understand that peace is not a program or perspective; peace is a person
- Embrace the gift of peace Jesus promises
- Slow down your busy life and learn to walk in the pace of Jesus
- Discover the distinctions of John's Gospel through context and historical insights

HOW TO WATCH YOUR VIDEOS

1. **Go to** my.lifeway.com/redeem **and register or log in to your Lifeway account.**

2. **Enter this redemption code to gain access to your individual-use video license:**

MY9XC6QDJTYM

Once you've entered your personal redemption code, you can stream the video teaching sessions any time from your Digital Media page on my.lifeway.com or watch them via the Lifeway On Demand app on any TV or mobile device via your Lifeway account.

There's no need to enter your code more than once! To watch your streaming videos, just log in to your Lifeway account at my.lifeway.com or watch using the Lifeway On Demand app.

ALSO AVAILABLE

eBook with video access, includes 7 intro teaching sessions from Melissa Spoelstra, each approximately 2-3 minutes

Bible Study for Women includes video access to 7 video teaching sessions from Melissa Spoelstra

Browse study formats, a free session sample, leader assets, and more at lifeway.com/gospelofjohn

QUESTIONS? WE HAVE ANSWERS!

Visit support.lifeway.com and search "Video Redemption Code" or call our Tech Support Team at 866.627.8553.